PRAISE FOR *CROS*

"I am humbled to write a few brief words for *Crossing the Line*... this book is a page turner, written in an honest and very visual depiction of a young white woman raised in a strict Mennonite household. Dorcas decided to move to the segregated South and shares her journey in her work experiences as well as her interracial personal relationships. Readers will enjoy a bumpy, truthful ride and a better understanding of struggles of Black/white relations in the South."

- Cheryl Holland-Jones, Community Advocate

"Dorcas Cyster's memoir, *Crossing the Line*, is a culmination of decades of life experiences, challenging oppressive systems, and embracing divine presence. This powerful narrative explores personal growth through family, church, education, and career, while confronting systemic racism and oppression and embodying wisdom. Dorcas addresses crucial questions about overcoming internalized oppression, navigating exhaustion from social justice work, and finding love amidst seemingly insurmountable challenges. Her story is a beacon of hope, pushing the boundaries of human endurance and charting a path towards healing and meaningful change."

- Althea Anita Banda-Hansmann, Diversity, Equity, Inclusion and Belonging (DEIB) Consultant, Coach, and Spiritual Director

"Dorcas was able to share her own story without judging others through her experiences. She did a great service to the reader. Thank you, Dorcas!"

- Thelma W. Horst, Retired Nurse, Mentor, and Author (Born to Be Adopted).

"This captivating memoir offers a deeply personal and powerful account of life in South Africa through the eyes of a white American woman. Married to a man of color during a time of profound social and political change, she provides a unique and heartfelt perspective on her experiences spanning over many years. Her story is a testament to resilience, love, and the human spirit. This book is not only a reflection of her life's journey but also an inspiration to all who read it."

- Dr. Makhale-Mahlangu, Clinical Psychologist in South Africa and Author (Phekolo-Afro-Centric Healing Modality for Rape Survivors).

CROSSING THE LINE

Crossing the Line

Challenging the Barriers of Race, Religion, and Relationships

DORCAS HORST CYSTER

PALMETTO
P U B L I S H I N G
Charleston, SC
www.PalmettoPublishing.com

Copyright © 2024 by Dorcas Horst Cyster

All rights reserved

No portion of this book may be reproduced, stored in a retrieval system, or transmitted in any form by any means–electronic, mechanical, photocopy, recording, or other–except for brief quotations in printed reviews, without prior permission of the author.

Hardcover ISBN: 979-8-8229-5922-4
Paperback ISBN: 979-8-8229-5921-7
eBook ISBN:979-8-8229-5923-1

CONTENTS

Preface   xiii

Chapter One: Sitting at the End of the Bench   1
Chapter Two: A Night with Shakespeare   14
Chapter Three: Forgiveness   26
Chapter Four: Crossing the Line   36
Chapter Five: Complicit   46
Chapter Six: Sexuality, Lies, and Love   61
Chapter Seven: Living Illegally and Other Contraventions   78
Chapter Eight: This is Not My War   90
Chapter Nine: American Citizen Born Abroad   101
Chapter Ten: Mama's Little Hope   111
Chapter Eleven: Community   124
Chapter Twelve: Life Together   136
Chapter Thirteen: For Better or Worse   152
Chapter Fourteen: Leaving Religion Finding God   172
Chapter Fifteen: Hope and Change   188

Epilogue   199
Acknowledgements   215
About the Author   217

Crossing the Line: "To overstep a boundary, rule, or limit" (Wiktionary)

"…behave in a way that is not socially acceptable" (Cambridge Dictionary)

DEDICATION

To my husband Graham and two daughters who have crossed barriers with me for the past thirty something years. I trust that the weight of traveling with me is not greater than the joy and maturity that I see in all of you. I loved you before I knew you and have no regrets.

Preface

I lived within bubbles of unfreedom many times in my life, restricted by my culture, religion, and race. I grew up in a sheltered, conservative white culture. My early years were shaped by the fears of the 60s: the Vietnam War, the civil rights struggle, and the assassination of J.F.K. and Martin Luther King. The Cuban Missile crisis loomed large, and the fear of communism was everywhere. In first grade we had air raid drills where we had to crawl under our desks. Later as I entered my teens, the 70s had a new spirit of defiance as the Vietnam War demonstrations increased and outrage grew over Watergate. The sexual revolution emerged, and women became more assertive for equal rights. My Mennonite roots were oppressive and stifled who I was as a woman: I began to change and challenge the oppressiveness.

I write about my family experience, knowing that it is my unique experience as the youngest of seven children. I write about my parents with tremendous respect for all they have taught me by actions and words. I have experienced both the fond memories and the painful experiences differently than my siblings. I write my truth and the impact it has had on my life.

I write with appreciation for the spiritual foundation I was given in the Mennonite church, knowing that while it has caused me great pain, it has given me strength. I know that religion is responsible for great happiness and great trauma for many whom I have encountered along the way. My hope in sharing my journey of recognizing what is life-giving and what is destructive may help those on the brink of questioning. Your God will go with you as you step into the unknown as She/He has with me.

I write with humility as a white person of privilege and power. I still need to fully realize what this means. I write of my experiences in the North and the South in the United States of America. My experiences with race were more overt in the South, not because the racism is worse there, but because I found it to be more blatant in the time period I was there. I am aware that oppression was and is more insidious in the North, cloaked in intellectual language and behavior.

In my writing I use the terms "white" and "Black" instead of African American and Caucasian. In my experience, persons of color have varied preference for use of these words as identifiers. My experiences in Mississippi were before the term "African American" was used. I also use the term "Coloured," for mixed race individuals during the years of Apartheid. This term is offensive to some South Africans who prefer to be identified as Black. Others identify themselves proudly as "Coloured" and reject being identified as Black. These terms remain socially and officially ingrained in the current South African context.

My decision to change and grow has taken me to places I could only dream of. As I opened myself up to build relationships that crossed racial lines, challenged my religious beliefs, and shook the very core of my being, I experienced life in a fuller way. I share my experiences in the hope that readers who seek greater freedom and ways to do justice for their own sake and others will be inspired to do the same. I come from very humble beginnings and yet the willingness to "go where others fear to tread" has brought me in contact with kings and queens of struggle and hardship. I have changed the names of some of these individuals, while others have given me permission to use their real first name. I owe each one a great debt.

My intent is to illuminate those places that religion, family systems, culture or race, and society often obscure by denial or ignorance. In doing so, great harm has come to our souls. Guilt and fear have stunted relationships and the ability to venture outside the walls we put around us to keep us safe.

CHAPTER ONE

Sitting at the End of the Bench

I had a reoccurring dream throughout much of my childhood. I am standing under a large maple tree outside of the country home where I grew up. As I look down the familiar dirt road that rambles past the cow pasture and large pond, I look farther toward the row of trees that outlines our small farm, still a special place for me. The trees are tall, yet taller still is a large brown bear, standing on its hind legs and looking around curiously. Even as a young child, I did not feel panic or overt fear associated with the dream but rather a sense of wonder and disquiet. As I began to walk down the road toward the bear, it receded into the atmosphere. In my dream I stopped and looked with some relief yet a sense of perplexity.

I forgot this dream for many years until recently when I began to think back over my life and the large challenges I seemed to be led into. I now believe this dream was one of many Divine communications that have been revealed to me years later in life at times when they were necessary reminders of God's faithfulness.

I believe the dream signifies that I would face challenges in my journey, sometimes bigger than I would feel I could handle. Yet even though they loomed large above the trees, I would walk toward them, and the scariness would dissipate as I entered the challenge. I had no knowledge of that at the time, however, I held this dream in my soul and never shared it with anyone until this writing.

I also believe that each one of us has a unique journey that we are called to. Often, we can only see the next few feet in front of us, and it is up to us to take the next few feet at a time. I now know that if I would have seen all the way around the bend in my life, I would probably not have taken the next few feet. That is God's grace.

My earliest memories begin in the country home my family moved to when I was about two or three years old. I was born in 1956 in Reading, Pennsylvania. My father believed he needed to move his seven children into the country for a more conducive environment in which to raise a family. As the youngest of seven, I escaped the initial hard work of developing the neglected thirteen-acre farm and accompanying primitive farmhouse into a habitable home. My courageous, strong mother worked hard with few resources to make a comfortable home that felt safe and nurturing. She knew I was her last child, and so she may have been extra attentive to nurturing my needs and wants. I know this played a crucial role in my solid foundation for life.

Those early years were filled with warm summers of berry picking, forest excursions, and swimming in the pond. The winters meant ice-skating, sledding, and hot chocolate. Especially important in my development were the two years that I was the only child at home while all my siblings were in school. For once I was the only one talking, the only one asking for things, and my words did not get lost in the shuffle of noise and clamor of my older siblings. I did not mind that my mother kept me out of kindergarten so she could have "another year with me" as she explained later when I inquired. She was careful to teach me what I needed to know, using her early childhood education background that she studied in college. My mother dropped out of college in her third year to marry my father and raise her brood, but education was important to her and gave her a sophistication that was unusual for the 1950s, especially in Mennonite circles.

I have memories of setting off into the woods that surrounded our property on more than one occasion with a packed lunch to sustain me. My mother would pack a peanut butter and jelly sandwich, homemade chocolate chip cookies, and a piece of fruit in a brown paper bag and off I would go. For a child of five, this was an exciting excursion. I never ventured too much further beyond where I could still see the reassuring farmhouse, but I felt independent and free. There was a particular large flat rock warmed by the sun where I would sit and spread out my lunch. I watched the birds' activity and the occasional chipmunk or bunny scurrying out of my way. Mostly I just sat and talked to myself, discussing all the important things that entered my young mind.

As I look back many years later, I believe that this is where I first met my God in a meaningful way. Even though I did not have the words for it at the time, my soul was communicating with her Creator. Despite not having much material wealth, I was immensely blessed with childhood security and love that served me well later in life.

Sometimes being alone had blessings, but it also called for creativity and imagination without siblings to lead the way. One day I decided I wanted to go fishing. I had neither a pole nor tackle. I decided that I would make it work anyway, so I found the handle of some type of farm utensil that served as a pole. I found some old fishing line but no hook, so I raided my mother's sewing kit for a safety pin and attached it to the fishing line. Shovel in hand I went to the garden to dig up fat, juicy worms for bait. I then set off to the edge of the pond where I knew my brother always fished successfully. It was not long before I had caught two or three "sunnies" as we called them. They could not have been longer than four or five inches in length, but I was determined to have them for my lunch. When I presented them to my mother with the request to fry them for me, she complied. The many duties she had as a wife and mother did not always render her this patient, so I must have caught her on a good day. I still remember eating those pan-fried fish, crunching the bones, and licking my fingers like they were the best thing I had eaten in a long while. This experience was a gift.

While it sounds like I had a perfect childhood, there were deficits, of course. The culture of the Mennonite church in which I was born, lived, and breathed multiple times each week was largely one of judgement for others outside of the Mennonite faith, and fear of sin and going to hell for that sin. On the other hand, there was tremendous security in the close-knit church family: I have many happy memories of church activities and dedicated women who nurtured me as a child. But as I was to learn, anyone stepping outside of the rigid dress and legalism lost that security. Mennonite doctrine at the time was full of judgement for sin, defined as worldly dress, worldly social activities, and worldly media in song, movies, and literature.

Mennonites fall into two distinct boxes: ethnic Mennonites and non-ethnic. Ethnic Mennonites can trace their history back to European ancestors who came to America to escape persecution by state churches. The non-ethnic box is a collection of all others who resonate with various aspects of the faith but do not have ethnic roots to Mennonite lineage. My parents were both ethnic Mennonites. Their ancestry, and hence mine, goes back to the 1700s when distant relatives came by boat from Germany and Switzerland.

Somewhere along the way a large group broke off from the Mennonite church, calling themselves Amish after the leader of the breakaway group. They remain a more conservative group, rejecting modern inventions such as cars, electricity, and public schools. The Amish are a more recognized group in public arenas with their culture being embellished and portrayed in Hollywood movies and society at large. Mennonites kept many aspects of the religious doctrine but have progressed over the years. Currently there are many branches of the Mennonite church ranging from those who wear conservative black dress to others who have no outward appearance that identifies them as Mennonite.

I was born into a moderately conservative church. Women were required to wear longer dresses of various colors and prints although red was discouraged, possibly seen as a "harlot's" color. Dresses included an extra piece of material sewed over the bodice for modesty, known as a cape dress. Women did not cut their hair, putting it up into some type of bun, with a head covering made of white netting required over this. The men wore dark plain suits buttoned up to the neckline without lapels and sometimes black, broad brimmed hats. However, this attire was for church services, so for the rest of the week, men wore normal clothing, and their appearance did not set them apart.

For me the paradox of my early church experience was the fact that the church I attended, and my father pastored, was smack dab in the middle of Reading, a midsize city in Pennsylvania. So, while I was exposed to non-ethnic Mennonites who came to our church, they either had to conform to dress codes and rigid doctrines or attend services without membership or the right to take communion. "They were allowed into the house but could not sit around the table," as my non-ethnic Mennonite husband phrased it after his experience with exclusion within the denomination.

At the age of six I began first grade in a public school just outside of Reading. My young classmates for the most part were kind and did not notice or care how different I looked. Even though my hair was combed and plaited into long braids, and I wore homemade dresses, I was largely accepted by fellow students and loved by my teachers.

My first memory of feeling set apart came with fifth grade May Day celebrations. The fifth graders always danced the May Pole dance. This required daily practices on the school playground preparing for the performance that parents and other school children attended. When I went home and told my parents about this, they informed me that they would write a note to the teacher explaining that I was not allowed to participate in activities that included dancing. My teacher kindly arranged for me to sit on a blanket at the edge of the playground with faculty members while the practices and performance was going on. I remember feeling slightly out of place sitting with the teachers on the sideline, but it did not disturb my sense of well-being.

As I moved through my school years, my parents wrote letters to other teachers excusing me from other activities that were considered "worldly." I sat alone in an empty classroom while all my other classmates gathered in the school auditorium to watch the movies *Romeo and Juliet* and *West Side Story* as part of the English curriculum. I remained behind at school while the rest of the gym class went to the bowling alley to learn to bowl as part of the physical education program.

At the tender age of ten years old, I responded to a fire and brimstone message from a traveling evangelist by going forward to the front of the church to acknowledge my sin and get saved from going to hell. I will never make light of the authenticity of those moments where I wept profusely and prayed the sinner's prayer. While my journey from accepting a judgmental and punishing God to discovering the magnificent and freeing love of God has been long, I do not deny the import of the origin of that quest. What was damaging came after that.

As a Mennonite pastor, my father knew the next steps after "accepting Christ and getting saved" were to be baptized into the Mennonite church. This meant putting on all the elements of plain dress that were designed to hide female anatomy and thus guard against male lustfulness. My father explained to the local bishop that it would be best for me to wait at least a year before going through with baptism and church membership as I was so young. So, at the ripe age of eleven, I began wearing the white head covering and cape dresses. My budding young breasts were covered by the cape dress and prevented male eyes from being tempted. The white head covering, according to Mennonite church leaders, was to show my submission to

God and to the men who were my Spiritual Head: my father, and whenever I got married, my husband.

While many deficits in my childhood years could be attributed to the patriarchal, judgmental, and legalistic culture of church life, my family system and culture also challenged my development. I think of myself as sitting at the end of the bench, both realistically and metaphorically. Literally, there was a long white bench at the dinner table, and I sat next to my mother at the one end along with my brother in the middle and my next older sister on the opposite end. The important stuff happened at the other end of the bench. My older sisters shared all their experiences in school and with friends, engaging in lively conversation with my father at the other end of the table. I was often caught up in squabbling with my brother, whom I loved or hated, depending on how accommodating he was to me, his kid sister. My role was often listening to the "wisdom" of the elder siblings. If I tried to offer a word or opinion, they often deemed it unimportant or did not even hear me.

Metaphorically being at the end of the bench meant often "catching up" with the rest, only to find that when I caught up and could share common experiences, the rest had moved on. Being the seventh child in a ten-year sibling range never gave me much opportunity to be the "cute little sis" who came on behind and everyone loved to tote around. My mother was often overwhelmed with all the chores and meals to prepare, so she often roped in my older sisters to comb my hair or bathe me, sometimes willingly, other times begrudgingly. As one by one my siblings left home, I began to realize the lack of depth of relationship I had with them. As a young adult, I began to skip family gatherings, instead hanging out with friends where I felt affirmed and significant.

Several years later, I left Pennsylvania and would not return for almost twenty years. When I returned in the mid-90s, I faced challenges in asserting myself within the family system. Even as an adult in my forties with more life experiences in diverse places in the world than any of my siblings, I struggled to feel recognized. I was still sitting at the end of the bench.

I received infrequent affirmation both from parents and siblings. As an adolescent, I developed a passion for horses and worked hard to draw them. My parents bought me a large blackboard. It stood in our family dining room and was my canvas for drawing. One of my siblings laughingly criticized my drawings of horses. While the words cut deep, I remained determined to draw horses more proficiently. However, I don't remember my family ever praising my efforts.

I had a childhood friend who shared a common passion for horses and other similar interests. She was not warmly received by my mother who seemed to find multiple things wrong with her and her family. In general, my family made critical comments about others as we observed people, their homes, and other aspects of life. Our targets were anything from "fat" people to "look at those horrendous Christmas decorations." I believe some of the critical spirit I was raised with came from anger and resentment at having to be different and Mennonite. It is hard to be kind and extend grace to others when a person feels consistently scrutinized and assessed for adherence to rules and regulations.

Paradoxically, those same parents, who sometimes gave conditional love, defied the rules of strict Mennonite teaching, and took us to the beach. We all were allowed to wear bathing suits purchased at stores, not handmade. I would jump the waves with my father, feeling so safe as he held my hands tight. In later years he would be admonished from the pulpit for this immorality by a more conservative preacher who took over his ministerial position when my father was promoted to bishop.

My mother introduced us to classical music and opera at an early age. I would sit with my brother and listen to long-play albums of *Peter and the Wolf* and other classics. One of my older sisters, and I knew the whole soundtrack from *Amal and the Night Visitors*, singing it as we did dishes together. Books were an important part of my home. I remember my father reading to me from the Book House Books series. These substituted for TV which was strictly forbidden by the church. Books took me to all kinds of places that I could only imagine and later introduced me to sexuality and passion. I credit my mother and her influence on my dad for exposing us to culture and intellectual stimulation. She was years ahead of many of her peers in the church. This atypical nurturing from my parents was a blessing and laid the foundation within me for resilience and strength to work through the painful stuff.

Years later as I processed my Mennonite upbringing, I became deeply angry. I had missed out on so much of what normal adolescence is supposed to be. I never had a boyfriend until my early twenties, and I never learned to dance. I never played a high school sport (oh yes, that was worldly as well). It would be years into my adult life before I actually dared to believe I was pretty. I still struggle with the need for affirmation and approval after all those formative years of rejection, isolation, and ridicule by peers when peer influence means everything.

What really was so harmful for a young ten-year-old girl to skip around a maypole on May Day, weaving pastel colored crepe paper ribbons? What harm was there in a young girl budding into puberty dressing in lacey dresses with flouncy skirts? What harm in being pretty and going to movies and sports events? Those questions all had answers back then from men in dark suits who made a rule book for particularly women to stay submissive and pure from the world... at what cost? To me those questions remain rhetorical because they are not even legitimate questions.

Someone recently asked me why I conformed to all those rules. What kept me from tearing up the excuse from the movies I was not allowed to see at school and attend with my classmates? Why did I not refuse to wear some of the Mennonite clothing? As I ponder this question, it comes down to one thing: control. The love and care that I felt from those who forced me to do these things prevented me from resisting. I needed that love, even though it depended on obedience to strict and legalistic rules. It was conditional love. I have spent much of my life unlearning conditional love and embracing unconditional love from my God, my husband, and many others who love freely.

The Horst Family Children (1956) from left to right: Margaret, Ellen, Naomi, Esther, Tom, and Nancy holding Dorcas

Dorcas' first grade school photo

CHAPTER TWO

A Night with Shakespeare

The inquisitive yet respectful attention to my different appearance continued through the sixth grade. I managed to maintain a sense of equilibrium as I carefully learned to navigate the delicate path satisfying religious demands and my own need for adolescent autonomy. As a young teen, fitting in is as necessary as the air you breathe. I developed friendships and was selected to be a school bus safety patrol which allowed me to try out my obvious leadership skills for the first time in the context of public school. My teachers liked me, and I did well academically. And then things dramatically changed.

The graduation from sixth grade into junior and then senior high school (that was before middle school existed) beginning at the age of 13 jolted me abruptly into a student body of over 1200 students. It was the era of American changes, emerging from the shameful 60s of civil rights struggle and assassination of its leaders into the "peace, free love, and flower power revolution" of the 70s. The inhibitions of the previous generation were struggling for freedom; nothing was sacred anymore and all was up for ridicule and question.

The impact that wearing religious garb had on my psyche at this age was significant. I was in the developmental stage of life when the import of peer support and acknowledgment supersedes that of parents and family. I continued to wear a white head covering, long cape dress, and conservative shoes and nylon stockings until after I graduated from high school. I found myself standing on the sidelines, longing to be invisible in my oddity. I felt lonely and rejected.

My school halls were a mass of movement and loud verbiage: 1200 students trying out romance, wearing miniskirts, smoking in the lavatories, exploring pot, banging locker doors, and the occasional physical brawl. I was drawn to the vibrancy of it all, yet aware of how far my reality kept me from fully belonging to it.

Several incidents of ridicule which I experienced will forever be in my memory, even now too painful to laugh about but just to accept as life lessons. I was in the midst of a busy hall, changing classes when one of my few guy friends came up behind me and pulled on my head covering. The white netting cap fell to the floor among the shuffling feet, and miraculously escaped being destroyed; I quickly retrieved it and put it on my head. My face was flushed red as overwhelming embarrassment washed over me. This incident was particularly confusing because for my friend it was a good-natured joke, but for me it was painful and began a pattern of isolation in my teen years.

Who could I trust to accept and stand with me as a friend? Would they stand with me despite peer pressure and ridicule? My natural inclination was to smile and reach out and let folks know how nice I was, and yet I was scared to be further humiliated by their rejection.

There was only one year that I overlapped any of my siblings in the same school building. All my older siblings left public school after tenth grade and attended a private Mennonite school. I attended public school for the whole 12 years. This was at my request to my parents because I reasoned that I was already an accepted oddity at public school, why break new ground at another school. Even though the school was Mennonite, the student body in no way reflected the conservatism my parents and church required of me.

When I was in seventh grade my brother was in ninth grade. One day, he was coming down the open staircase as I was going up. We were surrounded by students. I remember looking up and seeing him coming down and wondering what I should do. Would my own flesh and blood openly acknowledge me? He fit in with his peers, no distinctive clothing that identified him as anything but a young man with his friends. As we got closer, I tentatively glanced his way, not wanting to embarrass him by being related or associated with this little Mennonite girl. As we passed each other, he gave a furtive sideways glance of recognition before blending back into the stream of students.

I remember at the time not feeling anything unusual about this occurrence. I totally understood his reluctance to stand out and his own need to belong and be accepted. I do not remember ever speaking about the occurrence until we were both older adults. It was one of those painful areas that I needed to revisit and redeem. Tom is now a licensed family therapist and fully accepting and aware of the misogynistic practice of religion and how it has affected our family and the larger community. We have a close and open relationship that has grown from owning the past and all its pain.

Another incident that reinforced my desire to be invisible and escape laughing eyes was one that drew attention to the thick nylon stockings with seams down the back I was forced to wear. Marilyn Monroe may have looked sexy in such stockings but in the 70s these were a relic, and seamless pantyhose had taken the fashion world by storm. For some reason, seamed stockings were part of the Mennonite dress code for women, and hence for me.

I was sitting in study hall, in the back row as to have a vantage point of being able to see others, without giving them the opportunity to scrutinize me. It was over the lunch hour, and the long lunch line stretched down the hall past the open door of the room in which I was seated. One of the girls in line looked into the room and saw me sitting there (so much for the back row vantage point). She exclaimed loudly enough for her friends and everyone in the study hall to hear, "There is that girl with the big fat seams down the back of her stockings!" There were giggles from her friends and an uncomfortable hush in the room as the words drifted back to me…. alone, shamed, and wishing I was invisible.

Another time, I was exchanging my books out of my locker between classes when a very attractive popular girl came up to me and said hello. I was cautiously pleased at the acknowledgement from her and gave her my attention: my sense of isolation and desire for friends made me susceptible to overtures. She complimented my dress and said she would like to have one made like it, could I give her the pattern or tell her where I got it. I explained my mother made it, but I could get the pattern for her if she wanted it. My mind was wondering: why does she want a dress like mine? I began to suspect I was being set up as a dare or some other opportunity for ridicule;

this was confirmed as she returned to her friends across the hall, giggling as they walked off together. On the surface her question seemed almost a gesture of friendship, yet ultimately was a cruel ridicule of my plain-style dresses.

I had one true friend who remained faithful through high school and years after. Louise and I met soon after my family moved from my childhood home in the country to a small town in the same school district. I do not remember what circumstances drew us together but what kept us together was our mutual love of horses. I had to sell my old faithful bay gelding when we moved and was mourning my loss when she offered me the opportunity to ride her horse while she would join me with her sister's horse. This began a regular venture for the two of us. We stormed the streets of the small town, galloping up the long hill in the town center, drawing attention from bystanders as the horse's shoes hit the streets. Ah, life felt good in these moments.

There was another aspect that intrigued me about my friend Louise. She also was on the sidelines of the in-crowd, but she did not seem to care. She dressed stylishly and was attractive, but she did not strive to fit in with the popular kids. Louise had a mature social awareness that gave her a healthy skepticism of mainstream American values. She assertively expressed herself about inconsistencies she observed in politics, religion, and relationships. It could be a bit intimidating, but it fascinated me. She represented free thinking and unapologetic honesty. She challenged me sometimes in my less than forthcoming need for acceptance and affirmation.

I invited Louise along to some of my church youth activities. She participated but she also quietly observed some of the dynamics and topics of discussion and quickly picked up on inconsistencies with what was said and what was lived. She challenged the church principles of love, yet members refused to accept others unless they ascribed to certain dress codes or doctrines. Louise also noted pockets of gossip and criticism. While some of her observations were uncomfortable to hear at the time, I knew she spoke truth. Unbeknownst to her, the acceptance and friendship she afforded me during those difficult years was life-giving.

    Louise and I graduated together, and she is the only one I have a cap and gown photo with. We both became Licensed Practical Nurses. I was a bridesmaid in her wedding. I walked with her brother, arm in arm down the aisle, in a beautiful, stylish green gown. By that time, I was allowed to wear the dress for this special occasion. However, at the reception, sitting with my parents, when I was called on to dance with her brother for a special dance for the bridal party, I declined. That familiar humiliating flush came over my face as Louise beckoned me a second time to join them on the dance floor. I shook my head to indicate that I could not participate. Was it because my parents were there? Was it because even though I looked like I fitted in with my beautiful bridesmaid dress, an inner voice reminded me that I had never learned to dance and would make a fool of myself? I left the celebration soon after that. Louise never questioned me about that important day in her life when I certainly let her down. Many years later, we rekindled our friendship at a high school reunion. We remain friends and I respect her atheism, still appreciating her words of truth and challenge.

    There is another experience that seemed to be a culmination of all the years of feeling ashamed and conspicuous as a result of feeling set apart. In my early 20s I had developed a friendship with a young man. James indicated to me that for him the relationship was more than just friendship but while I could not share those feelings, I certainly valued the time we had together. He invited me to go to Philadelphia to see a Shakespeare play and I readily accepted.

As I got myself ready to go, I wanted to dress stylishly as befitted attending a Shakespeare play at a Philly theater. By then I had left the cape dress for more trendy fashions and my larger head covering had been replaced by a smaller one which was worn with my hair pulled back. I left my house and headed to Reading to pick up my friend James. On the way my mind toyed with the idea of taking off my head covering for the evening, allowing me to blend in with the crowd: just a normal guy and girl out for the evening. I did not take off my covering: my sense of integrity was too strong. If I had left the house that way, that would have been different, but sneakiness was not my way of doing things.

James and I entered the huge live-stage theater and found our seats. I was always glad to sit down in such a forum, feeling less conspicuous and part of the sea of faces. We chatted together, eagerly awaiting the opening of the play. We had excellent seats, and I knew they were carefully selected and paid for by James to ensure a great evening. Before long the music began, and the show had started. I was taken back to the days of Shakespeare's tragedies and enthralled in the characters that were developing on stage....

Suddenly, the reverie was interrupted by a sound like the loud yelping of a dog and as I drew my attention away from the stage to this intrusive sound, I realized it was coming from James, beside me. The next moments seemed frozen in time.... like a movie that got stuck in a scene that was not supposed to be there. The actors on the stage were momentarily distracted before their professionalism took over and lines were resumed. It felt like the stage lights and everyone in the house had moved their attention to the two seats where I and my friend were seated. James' body was contorted and contracting in what later I was to find out was an epileptic, grand mal seizure. I self-consciously recoiled from him; the element of surprise and the overwhelming feeling of being in the embarrassing spotlight rendered me unable to assist in his needs. Here was the Mennonite girl, trying to do something special, something normal, and of course she was with the boy who had an illness, a disease that set him apart and made him incredibly embarrassed and ashamed. What a pair!

What happened in the next few moments is still not clear to me; I dimly remember well-meaning folks reaching up from the seats behind us and attempting to get something into James' mouth to prevent his teeth from biting his tongue. I was well aware of this precaution as a nurse but was lost in my brief numbness of rational thought. There seemed to be a buzz of well-intentioned activity directed toward James, while questioning faces glanced my way, possibly wondering why there was no assistance from me, his companion. My first conscious thought was to get out of that place, that moment in time that rendered me in a spotlight of public humiliation. As the seizure ended and James sluggishly regained consciousness, I briskly inquired whether he could get up and walk, I indicated that we needed to get out of there-quickly. Miraculously James got to his feet and with my support, stumbled over folks to the end of our aisle, climbed the stairs to the top of the section, through the theater doors to a lobby and then out the main entrance to my car.

As I sat in the car wondering what now; my shame and embarrassment moved to anger directed toward James, who had not informed me that he suffered from epilepsy and the possibility of such an event happening. Not the kind of anger that made me want to lash out at him, but the anger that prompted a cool detached efficiency that inquired of him what needed to happen next; he obviously needed medical attention that much I knew. James directed me to a local hospital ER, where I remained in the waiting room as he was being seen. The kind, compassionate part of me that made me an excellent, caring nurse was still dwarfed by the cool and aloof Mennonite girl, sitting in a strange ER waiting room, reeling from the events that had happened in the last hour.

Later as I drove through the late-night darkness toward home, with James sleeping heavily beside me in the reclined passenger seat, I had a chance to think of what had just happened. There was a hollow, empty feeling in my gut, a feeling of more than just anger and embarrassment at the events that left me standing on the stage of speculation and anticipated ridicule. I felt in my soul a moral conflict; my own pain from past rejection and isolation, in the moment had prevented me from attending to my companion's desperate need for loving compassion in a humiliating, personal crisis. What kind of a friend did that make me? What kind of a follower of God?

The night of the Shakespeare play deepened my quest for personal wholeness. I wanted to discover who I was void of Mennonite identity. I wanted others to see me for what I was on the inside, not prejudged according to stereotypical knowledge. I wanted my soul to be shaped by love and to let my actions reflect that reshaping.

Months later it was time to move on. I gently ended my relationship with James. I had assisted him in finding a caring family physician who had stabilized his illness. James still felt there was more for us together, but I knew that life had another direction for me.

Sometime later, James took his own life. While I do not hold myself responsible for his tragic life ending, it was a time of deep pondering for me. I was attracted to James for his gentleness and compassionate heart. When we met, he was working at a half-way house for recently released inmates from prison. Sometimes our dates consisted of accompanying four or five ex-inmates on recreational activities. I enjoyed the exposure to young men of non-ethnic Mennonite background. James himself was not Mennonite. I do not know why James was attracted to me. The years of ridicule and lack of male interest instilled in me that I was unattractive and odd. Perhaps he saw something in me that I still could not see in myself that transcended my outward appearance or perhaps he did not care. James's life ignited a desire in me to afford others that same generosity and unconditional acceptance.

This was a difficult chapter to write. I revisited times in my life that generated feelings of shame and isolation that stayed with me well into my adult life. Most of these feelings have been redemptively processed and transformed into strengths, yet some pain remains as a distant reminder of a period of great "unfreedom" in my life. I also am aware that some of my sisters, both family and friends, continue to wear the "plain" dress of the Mennonite church. This chapter is not meant to be a judgment on their experience but rather a personal testament of my journey and how it affected me. I believe each woman must come to terms with the boundaries of her own religious journey and have the courage to do what is healthy for her.

Dorcas' seventh grade school photo wearing head covering and cape dress

Dorcas' high school photo in her senior year (graduated from Governor Mifflin High in 1974)

Dorcas Horst of Mohnton, Pennsylvania has accepted an assignment with Rosedale Mennonite Missions to Jackson, Mississippi. Dorcas is a daughter of Luke and Ruth Horst of Mohnton. After graduating from Governor Mifflin High School, Dorcas attended Rosedale Bible Institute and Reading Mollenberg Vocational Technical School from which she received a certificate as a practical nurse. She is a member of the Fairview Mennonite Church. She believes that the Christian life is one of giving, caring, sharing, and having a bond with brothers and sisters from all walks of life. She sees Voluntary Service as a way of reaching to others and of broadening personal experience. Her assignment includes nursing in a hospital and community outreach in the underdeveloped area of Jackson.

Newspaper article in hometown newspaper (Reading Pennsylvania) about Dorcas' plan to work in Mississippi. She is wearing nursing uniform and cap. (1979)

CHAPTER THREE

Forgiveness

Someone once said that you should need a passport to cross the Mississippi border. I now understand what they meant. In 1979, I went to Jackson, Mississippi, to work with youth in the deeply segregated South. I was going to work with a voluntary service program organized by the Mennonite church. I was drawn to Mississippi for some reason even though the director of the program tried to persuade me to work with the elderly in another state. He felt that the center in Mississippi was unstructured and volatile as it recently had experienced some challenges. I insisted that Mississippi was the place for me, so he reluctantly agreed.

Before I left Pennsylvania, I had a talk with my parents and informed them that I would no longer be wearing Mennonite attire. I wanted to do this with integrity and openness in respect of what they stood for, not to denigrate it by deceit. We parted with love and acceptance for each other. I would like to think they understood that part of my life had served its purpose.

I knew that something was changing inside of me. I knew that to cross over from following religious doctrines that made one "holy" to a lifestyle lived out of grace and freedom as God intended, I needed to leave home. I was a nurse by profession, but I also had a deeper call and that was to touch people's hearts and souls. To do that I needed to listen to my own soul and find myself apart from all the distractions that had buried the real me way down deep. I needed to do more than leave home: I needed to leave Pennsylvania.

As I gazed out the window of the van, traveling into Jackson from the airport, I noticed the change from interstate highway to beautiful suburbs with contoured lawns, and finally small houses with overgrown yards and abandoned vehicles in the driveways. This community would become my home. I was in West Jackson.

West Jackson was once a white community, abandoned by "white flight." I would later learn that this was a common phenomenon; as Black people moved into a slightly more prosperous neighborhood, white people would move out. This area of town now had a reputation for crime, drugs, and violence. The white community associated this with Black people living there and it was a no-go area for them. My white housefather, who was from the Midwest and rarely saw Black people, joked, "did you ever see so many Black people?" I thought that odd, as I was used to seeing diverse communities in Reading.

On one occasion I asked a white co-worker from the hospital where I worked to take me home as my car was being serviced. I was naïve at that time to the implications of what I had asked. As we drove closer to West Jackson, I sensed she was getting nervous. Upon inquiry, she informed me that she had never been to this part of town and did not feel comfortable taking me further. As the reality of the situation dawned on me, I eased her discomfort by suggesting that she drop me off and I would walk the rest of the way. She looked at me with a bit of disbelief and yet relief. It was one of my first experiences as being an ignorant "Yankee."

It was into this reality that I stepped out of the van and began my year of "Voluntary Service" or V.S. I had signed on to a year of working with youth in conjunction with a small Mennonite church. I was also expected to get a full-time job as a nurse. My income from nursing would be given to the Mennonite conference that sent me to Jackson, and in turn I would be given a small stipend to live on. The V.S. unit was a large house painted white with mainly white people living in it; it was called "the white house" by community folks. It is an example of the forthright honesty that the community extended to relationships and life in general.

This honesty was intimidating to me at first, but soon became a mirror for me to look at myself and see it as an opportunity to grow or to let it go and not take it so seriously. Most times it was an opportunity to see parts of myself that I was blind to. Sometimes it was just an angry youngster getting even.

There was plenty of anger and rightful distrust of white folks in the neighborhood. The children were innocent and loved the Bible classes and other activities that were afforded. The teenagers grew savvy, and it was harder to fake it with them. This was often the time when other volunteers and church members distanced themselves from the anger expressed. It was something I wanted to know more about.

I gravitated toward the older youth and had a girls' group of about nine or ten young women between the ages of twelve and sixteen. We had tremendous fun together, piling into my small Nissan and going to the pool, hot-dog picnics, baking cookies, and having open and honest discussions. Many of their peers at this age were already pregnant or heading that way. This was a big topic of discussion. I was open and accepting of their questions, often not having answers but hoping to build their self-esteem and open new possibilities for their future. It is due to their resilience and intelligence that all of them graduated high school without getting pregnant.

My naivete served as a blessing many times but I later realized that it could have easily been taken advantage of. It was a blessing in that I walked freely through the community where I lived unaware of deep, unsettled anger and resentment toward white people. My safety can be largely attributed to Black people's lack of penchant toward violence, even toward those who oppress and exploit them. History is replete with this truth.

That being said, as I was educated to the realities of the South, I thank my guardian angel for working over-time. I went to Jackson in 1979. In the preceding sixteen years, tragic events had occurred in the South and in the country that left those suffering under oppression permanently scarred. In 1963, Medgar Evers, a prominent Black Mississippi activist was gunned down at his home in Jackson, witnessed by his two small children. The sniper was an active member of the Klu Klux Klan and was acquitted by an all-white jury; he would finally be convicted in 2001 and died in prison. John F. Kennedy spoke out against the shooting. He was then assassinated in 1963, followed by his brother, Bobby Kennedy five years later. Then followed tumultuous years of resistance marches, beatings, and brutality against Black people as school integration began and lunch counter segregation was challenged. In 1968 Martin Luther King was brutally assassinated, leaving Black Southerners devastated. Almost every home in the impoverished community where I lived had portraits of Martin Luther King and John F. Kennedy on their walls. I can only imagine these served as emblems of hope through the years when the world seemed so hopeless and dark.

I developed a romantic relationship with a young Black man named Brayton. His mother lived in Brandon, Mississippi. This is a small rural town that has a history of lynching and brutality toward activists and Black people. While modern day lynching in Mississippi and elsewhere continues metaphorically as Black men continue to be killed and threatened disproportionally to white people, the last recorded physical lynching in Mississippi was in 1981.[1]

One evening Brayton asked me to ride with him to deliver a package to his mother. Brayton's mother had remarried after his father had died and Brayton was now living with his sisters in Jackson. He showed up after dark to pick me up. We talked and joked as we drove through the night but when we arrived at his mother's house, he asked me to wait in the car while he went in and interacted with his mother. Years later as I thought about that night, I wondered if his mother even knew he was dating a white girl and what she would have said had she known. I am sure she would have warned him of the dangers of a Black man dating a white woman in the South, let alone bringing her to the rural town of Brandon. She would have had memories of Black men/boys getting lynched for even glancing at a white woman. He loved her but only shared part of his life details with her. I only understood years later what was too terrible for him to tell me at the time. There were too many ghosts from the past that I had yet to learn.

---

1 The Washington Post, Lynchings in Mississippi Never Stopped, by DeNeen L. Brown (August 8, 2021)

This was the history of the community in which I moved so freely and unknowingly. A history that, if the roles were reversed and I were a Black person amongst white people so disenfranchised, I would not have had the same liberties. It is no wonder that I learned many important lessons from this community. Some loved me and a few hated me, yet all taught me so much about love and forgiveness.

Don was a fifteen-year-old Black youth. He was a frequent flyer at the "white house." Tall and lanky, he often taunted or teased the other youth playing ping-pong or basketball instead of participating. He could be as endearing to me as he could be challenging or belligerent. Many times, he addressed me using four letter words, and referred to me as a "hunky" who did not know anything (sometimes he was right). Often when he was endearing, he was high. His eyes and slightly slurred speech gave it away. One day he sauntered into the yard where several of us were playing ping-pong. He sat and watched for a while and then joined in by requesting "downs." This meant that he would play whoever won the next game. Unfortunately, he did not win the game that he played and he felt cheated. Instead of walking away he picked up one end of the ping-pong table and turned the table upside down, breaking the small netting in the middle. He then proceeded to tell us all off and walked away. The other young people were very upset at him and looked at me for support. I assisted them in righting the table, fixing the net, and then listened to their litany of words against Don.

This was not the first disruption that Don had caused in the back yard. I knew that it was important that the safety of the "white house" be preserved. It had a reputation of being a safe place for kids to play with supervision and parents were known to give their approval to their children's request to go out and play based on the fact that they were going to the "white house." On the other hand, I knew some of the challenges Don faced at home. His mother was a single parent of three children and worked long hours to make ends meet. His father had been incarcerated most of Don's life. Don struggled in school and with social skills. It was either go and speak to Don's mother or restrict him from coming onto the "white house" property. I felt that restricting him would be too harsh as it seemed it was one place that he enjoyed coming to. Several of us at the "white house" had started to befriend him and felt that this was a positive environment for him to gain confidence and grow. I plucked up the courage to go and speak to his mother. I tried to communicate to her that we wanted Don to come around but could not put up with his behavior as it affected the safety of others. She apologized for his behavior and then closed the door. The word got back to me from other children in the community that Don had gotten a "hiding" from his mother and a rather brutal one at that. I had no idea that my actions would result in such punishment.

The next morning, I walked outside to get into my car to go to work. I first noticed that my radio antenna was bent at a ninety-degree angle. As I walked around the front, I saw with shock that my front headlight was smashed as well as both side mirrors. I thought to myself, "who would do this?" As I sat trying to absorb the vandalism, the thought came to me that it may have been a retaliation for the action I took with Don. Several days later, the buzz in the community confirmed that indeed Don had been bragging about vandalizing my car. The youth from the community inquired as to what I was going to do. They advised me to go to the police and report him. I thought about it long and hard.

I was incredibly hurt. For the best part of a year, I had patiently put up with all this guy's abuse, forgiving again and again, continuing to include him in activities and taking him on outings with the rest. Yet he continued to berate me in front of other young people, calling me names, coming up in my face in a menacing way on occasions when I confronted him. And now this. Yet I still felt a check from going to the police. I knew that the justice system was stacked against Black youth, particularly if it was against a white person. I felt pretty sure that Don would be put in juvenile detention as this was not his first brush with the law. I could not bear to think of what his mother would feel with both men in the family behind walls of correction.

I did not call the police; I did not report it. I got my light and side mirrors fixed, using my little money from my stipend. Don never came to the "white house" again. I stayed in West Jackson but moved to another area and lost track of Don. A couple of years later someone told me that Don was in jail. I felt a great sadness. A life was wasted by poverty, loss of father role model, low self-esteem and all the disadvantages of being Black in Mississippi.

Bobbi was one of the first young people I met when I stepped out of the van from the airport. She was a precocious young Black girl of about twelve. She looked me over from head to toe, scrutinizing me carefully. She then proceeded to make comments of what she observed to friends around her. Again, that frank honesty about physical characteristics, none the least of which she found courage later to share with me. She called me "flat booty." I was to learn that this was not a compliment. An ample backside was considered sexy, and white women were often found wanting.

Bobbi was very dark skinned and within the Black community this was often a disadvantage and reason for ridicule. This was a remnant of slavery days when light skinned "Negroes" were given preferential treatment, and a phenomenon that still exists today. Bobbi was often the butt of jokes and called derogatory names that would highlight her color. I thought she had beautiful ebony skin, but that was little consolation for the pain of teasing by her peers. I sometimes would find her in tears and alone. There were challenges at home as well as her mother was very ill and stayed in bed for most of the day. Bobbi and I became friends. Our friendship endured through laughter, tears, outbursts of anger, and conversations that allowed her to open up about thoughts and feelings for perhaps the first time.

One of those outbursts of anger involved an altercation where Bobbi became very agitated because of a disagreement between us. There was a small stack of two by four planks on a pile in the yard that were going to be utilized for a building project. Bobbi became so angry that I was not giving in to whatever she wanted that she grabbed one of the planks and got a good lick in to my thigh before I was able to disarm her. Days later Bobbi returned to the white house like nothing had happened. We never spoke about the incident. The bruise on my thigh weeks later, served as a reminder of the anger that could destroy and hurt. I was determined to hang in there and demonstrate that love could overcome that anger.

Years later, Bobbi would be in my wedding and threaten my new husband that if he did not take care of me in South Africa, she would come and get me. Bobbi made me a cross-stitch wall hanging when I left America. It has my name, followed by the words from Psalms in the Bible, "I thank my God upon every remembrance of you." She signed the back with an inscription that indicates how she felt about our relationship.

Thirty plus years later, Bobbi is a survivor. She moved into a better community. Her determination to succeed financially and establish an independent family has been rewarded. She holds her own destiny in her hands today as she single-handedly parents five children and provides them with stable housing and a safe environment. Although we have been in and out of touch over the years, I know she will always have a place in my heart.

And me, I've learned a lot about forgiveness. I learned that I was able to forgive without being asked by the offender. I learned that to love unconditionally took a great amount of courage. I began to learn that sometimes we are called to do something with little or no comeback or appreciation. And that sometimes it is returned when we least expect it.

CHAPTER FOUR

Crossing the Line

The familiar icy fingers of anxiety tightened around my gut as I moved slowly along the cafeteria line. I robotically nodded assent to the questioning look of the cafeteria worker as she offered Southern fried chicken and lemon ice box pie, both specialties of the deep South. There were only minutes left before I would need to decide where to sit. In this situation, in Jackson, Mississippi in 1979 where social apartheid (segregation) was alive and well, there was much at stake. In the small private hospital where I worked, lunch time reflected this phenomenon. There were the tables where the white health care workers sat, most of them nurses and doctors. And then there were the tables where the Black staff sat, mainly nursing assistants and other non-professional staff. The forced cordiality required to render a working relationship in service to patients ended during the walk to lunch and social, mealtime conversation.

This particular day, I was delayed by a last-minute medication I needed to give before taking my lunch break. I had agreed to have lunch with several nursing assistants and a Licensed Practical Nurse (LPN) who went on ahead of me, informing me that they would save me a seat. After giving the medication, I informed the head nurse that I was going to lunch. She told me to wait for her as she was coming as well and so we walked together toward the cafeteria. I tried to engage in superficial conversation as we walked the short distance, but the internal battle had begun. I was certain that the white head nurse anticipated that I would join her for lunch with the other white professionals, but unbeknownst to her, I was already committed to joining those who had gone before who happened to be Black.

My heart said to do the right thing and join the Black staff at the table where they had saved me a seat. The importance of this act could not be underestimated. I had only been at the hospital for a couple of months and had witnessed multiple incidents of racist actions by white staff toward Black staff. I was determined to build credibility in my relationships with the Black staff to show that I was different. I wanted to demonstrate that our relationship superseded working together and that I could be trusted to be a friend. Having lunch together was an act of friendship. On the other hand, my white colleague that accompanied me to lunch expected me to join her with the other white staff. She knew her place in the equation, white Southerner, in power, mindful to be kind to the Black folks on the periphery and so necessary in preserving a way of life, but not to be treated as equal in the realm of social interaction. She felt confident in her place and free from conflicts concerning racial justice.

While my heart leaned toward integrity, the rest of me ached for the luxury of being able to fit in, to slide into that comfortable space and silence the voice of inconvenient truth. To sit where I was expected to and not stand out. But I knew that was just a fantasy. Even if I chose to sit with my "own kind," I would not fit in. For even though I could superficially enter their conversation, I would never be one of them. Nor did I want to be, but I cringed inwardly at being a spectacle for the whole lunchroom to see. The grip on my gut took me back to my high school days where my religious identity made me a spectacle in busy halls and classrooms. Then I just wanted to get to my next class unnoticed and without mocking words directed my way. Years later those scars remained.

I grabbed my iced tea, paid the bill, and turned to face the crowded dining area. I observed that seating was being adjusted for my colleague and me to sit with the white professional staff. I looked across the room to where another seat was vacant for me, and faces were turned in anticipation of me joining them. My face flushed as I informed the white nurse who had accompanied me to the lunchroom that I would sit with the others who had saved me a seat. She looked vaguely surprised and then turned away. I felt all eyes on me as I worked my way with lunch tray held high, across the seating area to the crowded round table where a seat had been saved for me. I was the lone white person around that table, and yet I did not feel excluded. I felt at home in the bantering and casual conversation and knew that I had done the right thing.

I was also aware of the questioning looks of some of the white folks as I turned away from where they sat. I suspect they did not understand the choice that I made and may have accounted it as this Yankee who did not understand how the South worked. For me the consequences for not meeting their racist expectations weighed much lighter than the hurt I would have caused in my Black co-workers. Nevertheless, I was glad when lunch was finished, and I could return to the safety of the restroom back on the medical unit. I went inside, locked the door, and sat down. I took some deep breaths and prayed. I told God that I could not go through that again. That I needed to draw a line in the sand as it were, so that when faced with similar situations there would not be a question. I would know what I needed to do and not waver.

Over the following months and years, I would discover how much I did not know or understand about the history of the South and more specifically about the institution where I was working. Following the lunchroom event, my relationships with the Black staff deepened and honest expression developed.

Mary, who was the LPN who saved me the seat in the lunchroom, later told me a story after she noted that a young Black man had dropped me off at work one morning. She pulled me aside later that day and said I needed to be careful. In response to the questioning expression on my face, she told me that about a year earlier there was a white nurse who was fired. Of course, other reasons had been cited but many of the Black staff attributed the underlying cause to be her open relationship with a man of color. Mary went on to say that she had no problem with my relationship, but white staff may feel differently. I shared more with her about the budding romantic relationship I was developing with the young man who brought me to work that day. I also said that if anyone was going to fire me because of that relationship, they would be in for a fight because they had no idea of how far I would take such a discriminating act. She smiled an accepting smile, but then softly added, "just be careful."

In 1979 most patients at this small privately-owned hospital were white, and I was to find out that it was only a year or more earlier that the institution had begun to admit patients of color. The reason I ended up working at this hospital was that they were the only hospital in Jackson that could give me exclusive day shift hours. This was important to me as a young woman who had other plans for my evenings and nights.

The interview for the job was one to remember. I met with Charlotte, the Director of Nursing, in a windowless office. We discussed my nursing experience as she chain-smoked Camel cigarettes. She hired me on the spot, and according to her never had any regrets. She was unphased by me being a "Yankee" as many Southerners were. Instead, she later asked me if I had other Northern friends who were nurses that would be willing to come south for a job. She was certainly one white person who did not fit into the white Southern female stereotype. Charlotte oozed a confident, assertive personality and spoke without flowery niceties or Southern drawl.

One incident that happened a short time after I began working there opened my eyes to the depth of suspicion and aversion to Black people that existed within many white people. I was assigned about twelve patients, all of whom were white. As I entered one of my patient's rooms, she called me over, motioning me to get closer, indicating she had something important and private to tell me. She informed me that she knew that one of the Black aides had used her hairbrush because there was "black, kinky hair in it." To her this was the ultimate offense, and the brush was now not fit to be used. I was so taken by surprise by all of this, that I went to the charge nurse and relayed what to me was a preposterous situation. I recovered the object of offense and presented it to her. There was no notable black hair as the patient had described. I assumed the charge nurse would go in and educate the patient that her accusation was unfounded. Instead, she questioned the Black nursing assistants about the accusation, which they flatly denied. The absurdity of it was obvious to me as the brush designed for white straight hair would never have worked for the unique needs of curly Black hair. Furthermore, I later found out that Black folks had their own share of distaste for white folks' hair. The charge nurse obtained a new brush and gave it to the patient, indicating that she had spoken to the offenders, and it would not happen again. I looked questioningly at her as she came out of the patient's room. She took me aside and informed me that I just did not understand how things were in the South between Black and white people. "It is different here," she added. This was an explanation I was to hear frequently over the next seven years.

Over the years I worked at deepening relationships with not only the Black staff but also with some of my white colleagues. I sensed in the charge nurse that I worked with that there was a softening toward me and a desire to be understood and accepted. Despite the hairbrush incident, we built a friendship of sorts. However, another incident reinforced my inability to grasp the distinction in white folks of not crossing the line regarding social interaction with Black folks.

One of the nursing assistants became pregnant. It was an unexpected but eagerly anticipated new life. Susan was older and had passed on to others many of the baby items she had from her other children. By this time, I had an open friendship with her and another nursing assistant. We joked and conversed freely. In my nursing capacity I always spoke respectfully as I requested duties to be done, often assisting with their allocated tasks when they were busy. It was into this relationship culture that I informed Susan that I would love to have a baby shower for her. She agreed and was grateful for the offer. Weeks later as we were discussing the invitation list, I mentioned that I was going to invite the charge nurse. In my mind she appeared to be softening to some of the social barriers that separated Black and white. When I informed her of the baby shower and that she was invited, she appeared to agree to attend. Susan and her peers smiled knowingly at me when I informed them that I had invited the charge nurse. They laughed gently and let me know that she was not going to attend despite what she may be saying. I insisted that I thought that it was going to be different this time, she seemed so genuine in her interest.

As the months went by Susan's due date was approaching as was the date of the baby shower. The Saturday arrived. I decorated my house, prepared all the food, arranged space for the gifts, and seating for guests. Susan and all her peers arrived as did the Black LPN we worked with but no charge nurse. As I checked my watch, I excused her lateness on getting mixed up with directions on this side of town and insisted she would come. Again, Susan and her friends smiled knowingly. When thirty minutes and then an hour went by with no charge nurse, I looked at them with resignation and disappointment. They were kind and assured me that it was a great baby shower, and we should just enjoy our time together.

As I pondered over the event that evening, I couldn't help but wonder... did Susan and her friends really mean that all was fine, was there not a shred of disappointment in them for the divides that continued to separate and deem them inferior of social interaction with white people? Was it enough that one white person tried to bridge the gap? I never got the answer to those questions. But I did get a deepening of relationship and truth building with Susan and her friends. That had to mean something.

I ended up working at that small hospital for seven years. I saw the hiring of the first Black RN, who ended up being the new charge nurse on my unit. I also worked with another Black RN when I began working night shift to complete my RN degree. She was from Texas and had more assertiveness with white folks. We became friends. One time she was washing my hair after coming to my home and giving me a henna hair treatment. She informed me that her mama was wrong, "white folks' hair does not smell like dog hair when it gets wet." We laughed.

I remember the growing number of Black patients who received care as the facility became more integrated. One older Black man I will never forget. He was transferred from a more rural hospital for treatment. When I entered his room, I witnessed fear in his eyes. Perhaps he was remembering a time when medical research abused Black bodies without consent such as in the Tuskegee Experiments in Alabama; this experiment utilizing Black men as subjects was not officially ended until the early 70s. [2] His fear was directed at me as a white professional, a troublesome reminder of how much damage was done to the bodies and souls of Black folks by white people. Times were changing, but the memories of these events instilled lasting fear and damage in many hearts and minds.

I would like to believe that even some of the white staff saw something different in me, that was not to be feared. I never succeeded in developing significant relationships with any of them outside of work. They had never been to my side of town and had no desire to go there. I lived where only white

---

2   Center for Disease Control and Prevention, The U.S. Public Health Service Syphilis Study at Tuskegee, cdc.gov, last reviewed 4/22/21

folks who were too old or too poor remained, secluded behind high fences, fearing the encroachment of Black neighbors. My white nursing peers tolerated my different ideas and respected my work ethic. However, when conversation got too uncomfortable and demanded reciprocal actions, they always receded into the white Southern mentality where there was power and control. Southern hospitality always had limits, I found out.

I have much to be thankful for from that small private hospital that took on this Yankee nurse with "radical" ideas. They acknowledged my quality nursing practice by awarding me two nurse excellence awards. These awards came with monetary value that assisted me in obtaining my RN license. I moved into a leadership position and honed my nursing skills with the guidance of my supervisors. But equal to the nursing and leadership skills were the lessons I learned from navigating the painful and confusing racial complexities of relationships at work and in social interactions.

Thirty plus years later, on one of my return trips to Jackson, I was perusing the grocery store with a friend who I was visiting. Out of the corner of my eye, I noted someone who looked familiar. I circled around because I did not want to make the wrong assumption of someone I believed looked like Susan. Then, I was sure. I tapped her on the shoulder and asked if she remembered who I was. She laughed and gave me a hug, exclaiming how could she ever forget me. She then asked me to wait, she had someone she wanted me to meet. She introduced me to her daughter, the one that she was pregnant with at the baby shower. We smiled together and reminisced about people we knew and what they were doing. The import of the occasion escaped her now grown daughter, but not the two of us. We knew, even on that day, many years later, the sight of a Black woman and a white woman hugging and conversing like long-lost friends in the middle of a busy grocery store was a rare sight. This was a story that started long ago and had impacted both of our lives.

The slow journey down the cafeteria line seems a lifetime ago. But the memory has served me well as a reminder of what I committed that day. For me, that day was a defining moment that affected decisions for the rest of my life. Though there would be times of faltering and longing for compromise to be able to fit in, I like to believe that truth won out most of the time. That first day when I "crossed the line" my inner being was called to truth and justice, and though there would often be angst within me, I would be faithful to that call.

CHAPTER FIVE

Complicit

White folks hate to be called racist. We pride ourselves on being wise, educated, and tolerant. Even though we hold all the power in most situations, we see ourselves as magnanimous, fair, and just.

That was me, though very unconscious of the fact. Many of us can go through our whole lives with this delusion as we do not allow ourselves to cross the line into equity of power with persons of color. It takes having one or more equal relationships or friendships with a person of color, or even more effective, serving voluntarily under a person of color in leadership, for this underbelly to show. A commitment of time to this relationship is also key. As in any other relationship the initial stages are a honeymoon period. As time goes on, the real differences come out when people face challenging experiences. In my experience, it is extremely difficult for a white person to stick around after challenges arise that reveal deep unresolved issues with white guilt, learned/unconscious biases, anger/fear, and benefits of white privilege.

The seeds of awareness were planted in me in Reading, Pennsylvania when I attended a predominantly black church on the "other side of the tracks." I developed a relationship with the

Black couple who were pastoring that church. Through our conversations, my eyes were opened to racism they had encountered living in Reading. They had difficulty in acquiring a mortgage to buy a home in a certain area that was predominantly white. They lovingly educated me to other realities of racism in Northern cities. However, when I went to Jackson, Mississippi, it was as if I emerged out of a grey fog of white unknowing within my own country. Initially my first response to this naked truth about myself and my culture was one of rejection. I was different, I had Black friends in Pennsylvania, I was "color blind."

Indeed, many of my early experiences with white Southerners confirmed that I was different. I saw the raw racism that existed in their actions and words and knew that I did not share the history of the South that so jaded them. However, several years later I was caught up in a movement that shook me to the core. It brought me to the pinnacle of whether I was going to stay and open myself up to the pain of a deeper racial conversion or back away into the comfort zone of whiteness. I chose to stay.

In the spring of 1981 after completing my 18 months of voluntary service and work with the Mennonite Church, I began attending a church called Voice of Calvary (VOC). VOC was a multi-racial/multi-ethnic church affiliated with a community ministry by the same name. At the time, mixed racial churches were a rare phenomenon. It stood out as a beacon of hope or disgrace, depending on who was observing. I well remember the curious stares of passersby as they observed this racially diverse group standing around talking, while children of various colors ran around playing after the service. It appeared all was well, and we were one big happy family. It was not so.

While there were great community projects and even social interaction between regular attenders, there was an imbalance of power. Most of the leadership was white, and those young people who had been part of the church for years were now young adults and were noticing and talking about that imbalance. They were a new breed of young Black men and women, having survived the civil rights struggle, integrated all-white schools, and grown in confidence as leaders. Several of them organized and approached the church leadership. What resulted will forever be known by those of us who participated as "The Reconciliation Meetings." It was a tumultuous time.

I cannot overstate the impact this time of necessary turmoil had on my life. I had left the small Mennonite church due to perceived lack of vision and paternalistic attitude toward community folks. I truly felt I had found a church in VOC that represented the community and its best interests. At first, I resented the interruption and decided not to attend the meetings. I wanted to believe that what appeared on the surface was true and that my sense of racial harmony was everyone's reality. I spoke to my brother-in-law, Spencer Perkins about it. Spencer, who is Black, married my sister who had joined me in Mississippi. He was (deceased in 1998) the oldest son of Dr. John Perkins, author, pastor, and civil rights activist. My history with Spencer has been a blessing and a challenge. Spencer told me to go to the meetings.

One evening I snuck into the meeting and sat on a chair at the back. I wanted to have an escape route in case it got too heavy. Things were being said by assertive and passionate young Black men and women, things that were hard to hear, things that I wanted to disassociate from. Accusations such as "white people have to always be in control," and "white people think their leadership style is superior." I wanted to stand up and say, "that is not me, I am the exception, I do not do that." I went away perplexed and feeling pain inside.

I went back to Spencer and told him what I felt. His abrupt answer was, "You need to keep going until you no longer want to make excuses or feel defensive." Because of my respect for him and because I am forever wanting to do the right thing (what a pain to have this in my DNA), I kept going.

Initially I felt shocked and stunned by Spencer's words. I thought he would absolve me of guilt and tell me I was the exception to the rule about white people. I remember several weeks of darkness as I wrestled with the guilt. I saw myself as a caring person who went into nursing to heal people, how could I be part of this pain people were experiencing? How could I ever fix this? How could I make it all better? I prayed.

Slowly, a dawning began. I began to accept responsibility for my history that was part of the history of the fabric of America. It was a history of domination and enslavement. It was a history of economic wealth at the expense of brown and black people, going back to the "founding" of this country. I grieved for the knowing and the unknowing. I grieved for the opportunities I had at the expense of others. I grieved for the ignorance of my parents and grandparents, and their parents, and so on. I grieved for the injustice that continues to permeate every aspect of society. I did not feel defensive anymore. I accepted my place as a member of the dominant population group in my country. However, it did not need to define me. I could rise above it, and while I will always be white and therefore a symbol of oppression to some, I could choose to live differently and work to the best of my ability to right the wrong. Spencer's dramatic challenge to me to stay with the process at VOC has been one of the milestone markers of my life.

I wish I could say that Kum Ba Yah happened after that in the church. Unfortunately, it was not that simple. As Black folks stepped into positions of leadership, many white folks left. "White flight" happened in the church. They felt "God calling them to other places." Sometimes I wonder how God feels about getting blamed for our stuff. It is very difficult for us as white folks to serve under Black leadership. White control seems to be in our DNA, especially for white males. This paradigm shift is so difficult and yet so necessary for trust building and providing examples of fair and just institutions. It is extremely difficult for the dominant culture to have to change their ideas of what will and will not work and trust the process of a different cultural leadership style.

The church did survive however, and in fact grew for years after that. Deeper conversations happened, as those who withstood the storm committed themselves to deeper community together. I remained at VOC until I left for South Africa almost five years later. My experience there remains the best example of what institutional church can be in America.

I cannot minimize the importance of white folks staying. It takes years, some may say a lifetime, for trust to be built between persons of another race. This is especially true if there is economic disparity as well. White privilege affords folks many more options. Often white Northerners would come to the South and work for a while, some with very good intentions. They would form relationships and then in a couple of years, move on with little thought of how that would impact those with no option to move out of their disadvantaged situation. It is hard to know what the answer is because sometimes short-term volunteering is necessary. I only know from my experience both in Mississippi and in South Africa that the gaping hole that is left after that person leaves begs a question of who benefits more from that experience.

My friendship with Dessie which has lasted more than 40 years bears testimony to the importance of staying. We met soon after I arrived in Jackson. She was cute and had a sassy side to her that I liked. I also saw the potential in her to succeed in life despite the social challenges she faced. She was particularly suspicious of white people; they came so often to the White House, stayed for a time, and then retreated to the safety of their northern suburban communities. She was one of 16 children, who happened to be one of a set of triplets. Dessie lived with her mother and siblings in a deteriorating small "shot-gun" house: if you stood at the front door, you could see straight back to the back of the house. The floorboards were rotting in some places with blades of grass pushing their way up through from the ground underneath. I spent considerable time in that home and even spent the night. I shared meals with the family. Dessie was/is a wonderful cook. She prepared her specialty of fried chicken, rice and gravy, and green beans, giving her best to this white girl. The occasional mouse running over the table and roaches on the wall paled into insignificance as I rested in the privilege of developing trust and community with her and her family. I knew that being with Dessie in her home, in her space, out of my comfort zone, would build that trust.

Dessie's mother was a strong, formidable little woman. Standing about five feet tall and skinny as a rake, she demanded and received the utmost respect from her children. In her home, she was the queen and everyone jumped at her command, with a "yes, ma'am." Outside of her home, life was hard. She was at the beck and call of white folks at her work. She cleaned rooms at a local hotel and came home worn and tired after working long hours to put food on the table for her large brood. I was scared of her. She tolerated me in her home. She did not make eye-contact with me which I later learned was forbidden with white folks when she was growing up. She seemed angry all the time. I kept hanging around, careful to stay out of her way, and to address her as "ma'am." After several years, I think she realized I was not going anywhere. She tentatively began to include me in conversations.

One evening with Dessie and her mother stands out in my memory. I was no longer living right up the street, but still in West Jackson, and I used to come by regularly to see how everyone was doing. It was one of those hot summer evenings when all you can do is sit on your front porch and hope for a small breeze to come along. There we were together, eating watermelon and drinking Kool-Aid. As we laughed and talked about nothing and everything, I felt a strange sense of community and privilege to be part of that moment. Me, a white girl from Pennsylvania felt humbled that a family so devastated by oppression and racism had allowed me to be part of this intimate, everyday event. There were other times when conversation flowed so freely, jokes were made about white people, and I had no problem laughing along. This was only possible because I stayed, and Dessie and her family demonstrated graciousness in seeing past my white skin and trusting my heart.

I not only stayed, I returned. Even after moving to South Africa, whenever I visited Jackson, I made it a point to spend time with Dessie and to visit her mother. On one of my visits Dessie informed me her mother was fighting a battle with cancer. I noticed how frail she looked despite her welcoming smile. In all the years we knew each other I had never felt free to hug Dessie's mother. I never took for granted the need for personal space between black and white distrust. Touched by her vulnerability, I instinctively stooped to hug her before leaving. I could feel the wasting of flesh on her small frame as she relaxed into my hug. I hugged her extra-long and said I would keep her in my heart. There was a certain peace about her, and Dessie confirmed that her mother had made peace with her God. It was the last time I saw Dessie's mother. She left this world to meet a world where justice is perfect, and rest is for all. Sometime later when Dessie and I were talking about her mother, she informed me that her mother had commented after our last encounter, that she had never been hugged by a white person until then.

Dessie often told me I had a black heart. I know she meant this as the ultimate compliment. I know however, that try as hard as I do, there is always the potential that this heart can still do damage from ignorance and white arrogance. There are times when I call her on the phone and think I am doing her a favor by reaching out. Frequently she ends up giving me a bit of encouraging wisdom for something I am going through. Sometimes she says, "I am going to pray for you right now" and she does, over the phone. And it is just what I need. It is God's grace and our love for each other that has sustained the integrity of our relationship through the years.

During the seven years I lived in Jackson, Mississippi, I lived in West Jackson, an area known for high crime. It became integrated in the 60s and 70s as Black folks gained more economic opportunities and desired better housing. Subsequently, white businesses and residents moved out. All my neighbors were Black or white folks intentionally living in communities of color. My white skin and big black Labrador dog afforded me a bit of privilege and protection from vandalism but not from the shared creatures that infested most lower income housing. Like most residents in the area, I was a tenant who paid a white landlord monthly rent. I shared the back end of a small house that was made into a very small apartment. The family of two parents and three children in the larger, front part of the house were Black.

There was a small stove that came with the apartment. To my dismay when I turned the gas on to cook, a host of roaches crawled out of the burners. The same thing happened when I attempted to use the oven. I tried scrubbing the stove and oven, believing only people who are unclean have roaches, but to no avail. The stove was so old and rusted almost everywhere that for as long as I lived there, I had roaches in the stove.

The roaches were not the only unwanted residents of my apartment. One cooler morning I reached up on my high closet shelf to remove a warm sweater that had been stored there through the summer. As I began to pull the sweater down, suddenly I felt squiggly creatures on my face, shoulders, and neck. I gasped and screamed when I realized that I had disturbed a nest of baby mice as the pinkish, grey creatures fell to the floor. I freaked out! I called my brother who lived next door (one of those intentional white people living in a community of color) to come and get rid of the mice. He came immediately and cleaned out the nest, discarded the sweater and I'm not sure what happened to the baby mice, probably better that way. I reported the occurrence to my landlord. He set some traps, but days later there were still mice. I reported it again. He put poison out, and there were still mice. I finally said that I was sure if I had mice, the adjoining apartment certainly had them as well, so they were probably just moving between the two apartments. I then stated that if the mouse problem did not improve, I was not going to pay my next month's rent. He then acted to have both apartments treated for pests. Things got better after that.

I would like to believe that had the same scenario played out with my Black neighbors and they complained that the same course of action would have been taken by my landlord. Reality tells me probably not. I had only lived in the apartment for a few months and they had lived in the other apartment in the house for years, accepting the unhealthy conditions. I know I had leverage with my white skin and privilege to defy white authority that my neighbors of color never had. I wonder if my landlord and his family would have lived in similar conditions. Conversely, my future husband was impressed that as a white person I would intentionally choose to live in these circumstances. This was the apartment I lived in when we met. In reality, I could not have afforded much more than this as I struggled to feed myself and my dog while in college and working part time.

It was a familiar sight to see white men roaming the Black community of West Jackson, logbook in hand, collecting revenue from rental units. To be fair, some units were maintained well on the outside but many others were run by slumlords in terrible condition. Local banks often denied mortgages to Black people, so these rentals served an unfortunate reality. There were a few community groups buying up some of these run-down homes and refurbishing them for low rent to own programs.

Staying and sharing life in a diverse community enables people to understand and come to terms with the racism in their own context. This is imperative if we want to freely engage with diverse communities effectively. It is often easier to acknowledge racial issues in other countries than recognizing them in our own backyard. One encounter with a volunteer from Australia, who came to Jackson to work with VOC ministries, has never left me and is a stark reminder of this cultural blindness.

I never saw "Aussie" (this was how white folks collegially referred to him) interact or socialize with Black folks from the community, but he was a great hit with white folks. I interacted with him infrequently but happened to be at a social event one evening and found myself sitting beside him. Wanting to have conversation of substance, I asked him if there were any racial challenges in Australia. He paused briefly, and then said, "No, there are only Aboriginal Indians, and they mainly live in the mountains, we don't interact much." He abruptly changed the subject, and our further conversation was brief.

At the time I was ignorant to the full significance of his statement. Sometime later I was educated to the tragedy of the treatment of the Aboriginal people in Australia.[3] By that time "Aussie" was gone from Jackson. I am not sure if I would have had further conversation with him if I had the chance, however I have never forgotten the blindness he revealed. Also, this white Australian showed such arrogance, coming to America's deep South, working in a community ravaged by the history of slavery and oppression, without owning the unjust racial history in his own country.

Each country has its unique challenges. Recognizing and opening to those challenges is a choice. But we dare not speak into other country's racial or economic challenges if we have not looked squarely at ours. Western countries seem to know best how to solve the world's problems. Unfortunately, it is these same Western countries that have created much of the world's problems. I needed to see and own the shit in my own back yard. It was difficult and painful. It made me sad and angry.

---

3   Movie: Through the Rabbit Fence

Why did I not know about this? Why had my parents not told me what was happening in my own country? Why had I been cocooned in white, apolitical, kind of Republican, Mennonite bliss? Why did the gospel I was raised with not speak into the injustice and oppression that was affecting my brothers and sisters of color? I felt I had only lived on one side of life and indeed I had.

Initially I wanted to go back up north and tell everybody off. And I did. It just so happened that this experience of enlightenment happened in my 20s, when the knowledge of youthful awakening to life's realities is often sidelined as naivete by older folks. I was breaking out of Mennonite bondage at the same time, giving me extra impetus to tell everyone to wake up and see what the real issues were in the world. Needless to say, my family was less than enthused about my new-found enlightenment. One of my sisters recently revisited this time in my life in an email she shared about modern day prophets. She honestly shared the reality of how our family reacted to new, uncomfortable truths of race in America:

> This [writing about modern day prophets] reminds me of a time… when Nancy and Dorcas came up from Mississippi, we were all (family members) sitting in a room together and the two of them were talking about their lives, speaking truth about racism, calling it out. It was not well received by some of us, voices were raised, the defensiveness was thick. I'll never forget it. They were two prophetesses, unwelcome in their own country. They were two courageous women, talking about the 'untalkable'.

This affirmation, forty plus years later, means a lot to me. At that time geographical distance served me well as I continued to grow in my understanding of the great divide between what I call my racial conversion and those who chose to remain blind. Over the years I found different ways to share my experiences and changes that were happening in me. Today within my family there remain varying levels of understanding on these issues based on levels of their individual experiences and relationships.

Having the scales of "color blindness" removed from my eyes was not fun. I owe my sight to seven years in Mississippi, the individuals who tolerated and loved me, and the grace of God to persevere. There were times when I lost my joy. I felt I was losing part of myself. On one of my visits home, my father asked me if I was happy. He had noticed my change in attitude and attributed it to loss of happiness. I thought for awhile and answered him that I really did not know if I was happy but I was sure there was joy and purpose somewhere. Pretty deep for a young woman in her mid-twenties, right?

It is a necessary part of life to go through metamorphosis at various times if you want to be effective and grow into the purpose for which you were created. Metamorphosis requires death. You can only become a different person if you are willing to die to old ways and belief systems that are no longer life giving. That is what happened to me in Jackson.

I had entered into uncertainty, darkness, and a community that was unknown to me. I had a choice to cling to what I knew to be true at that point or allow myself to be molded and shaped by a new truth. That new truth retained elements of the past but opened up whole new possibilities. I crossed over the line from not knowing to embracing all the pain and suffering that was part of the tragic history and present reality of America. Having done so not only allowed me to be a more authentic person but also brought new and exciting relationships into my life and forever changed me.

Dorcas in Jackson, Mississippi with her friends Dessie (right) and Bessie (left) after a Sunday morning church service. They are two of a set of triplets.

Dorcas' sister Nancy and brother-in-law Spencer Perkins (married in 1983)

CHAPTER SIX

Sexuality, Lies, and Love

My family did not discuss sex. It was not a negative, it just was not part of our family conversations. I suspect this may have been largely the typical family experience in the fifties and sixties. Added mute influence on this subject was the heavy-handed influence of the Mennonite church on such matters.

I do remember the sparks that went between my mom and dad when they kissed in front of us kids, sometimes my dad playfully grabbed my mom and held her tight. She would pretend annoyance but could not hide the little smile on her face as she gave in. I also remember sometimes at night, hearing my parents' door being closed. I knew then to knock before entering if I had a late-night need. Occasionally I would hear laughter emanating from their room through the partially opened door, giving me a sense of well-being as I lay in my bed in the room across the hall that I shared with two of my sisters.

I gained a sense of how procreation happened by observing the animals on our small farm. I knew we needed a ram for my pet ewe to have lambs. I knew that my female cat somehow got a big belly from the passing tom, but never witnessed the process. I still don't understand the whole chicken thing and fertilization of eggs! But I accepted that something happened between a male and female that generated new life. That was the extent of my childhood knowledge.

Having five older sisters that all entered womanhood before me afforded me an opportunity to learn by observation. There were no educative conversations with me from them or my mother. I remember the odd reference to buying "cornflakes" to my questions about the special stops at drug stores to buy sanitary pads for them. My curiosity as to the strange little toilet paper wrapped packages in the trash got the best of me. I was the designated trash can collector for the household. I collected and burned the paper trash regularly. One day I decided to open one of the curious little packages. This is how I learned about monthly periods. Somehow it did not alarm me to see the dried blood on the white pad, I just accepted this as a female process that I would one day experience and hopefully learn more about.

Most of my education on human sexuality came through the public-school system. Thankfully that was before the conservative evangelical influence prohibited sex education in public school. I had an informative, excellent education on female and male sexuality as well as related sexual diseases and contraceptive methods. This began in fifth grade and was appropriately graded until junior high. I still use this in defense of the public-school system and their ability to educate youth effectively and objectively on matters they may not get at home.

The Mennonite church was not just mute on this subject but tended to shroud all matters of sex in negativity and shame. The Mennonite attire that I was forced to wear only further reinforced that my female sexuality was bad and needed to be disguised under dresses with extra material over my breasts and down below my knees. Any attractiveness that I would ever see as I stood before a mirror needed to be disturbed by austere hair covering and garments that aged me well beyond my years.

My dating experience in my teen years was nonexistent. Any sexual arousal came from steamy novels that I consumed voraciously after trading my Black Stallion books for Frank Yerby novels and others that captivated me with stories of love and passion. In my late teens I defied Mennonite taboos by going to the movies with a girlfriend. I remember entering the glitzy cinema with mirrors lining the foyer. For a moment I hesitated at the multiple reflections of myself under bright lights entering this place of iniquity and sin. Leaving the bright foyer and entering the dark, intoxicating theater, I ate my popcorn and was enraptured by the movie *Grease*. Still today this is one of my favorite movies, not primarily because of the content although I love the music, but because of what it broke free inside of me.

The brief "romantic" relationships I had before I left for Jackson, Mississippi were indeed brief and unromantic for me. Those I seemed to be attracted to were not attracted to me and those that were attracted to me I was not attracted to. Hence while others were experiencing first kisses and romance, I was feeling rejected and asking myself what was wrong with me. I now am thankful that I did not get involved in a relationship that would have kept me from moving out of Pennsylvania and discovering all the adventures that were in store.

As with all other aspects of life in the South, there are overt racial dynamics to sexuality. The history of slavery has left its indelible mark particularly the sexuality of Black males and how white folks perceive it. The Black male was deemed almost animal-like in mentality and in sexual appetite by many white folks, while the Black female was often seen as more desirable especially by the white master. There is a whole psychological and social history that is very important to understanding this phenomenon to which I leave to the experts but would encourage readers to explore.

One early experience I encountered several months after being in Jackson, which would have been in the early eighties, educated me to the shocking and disturbing psyche white folks still carried. I was engaging in informal conversation with several of my co-workers as we sat in the nurses' station at the hospital where I worked. The topic of conversation was about one of the news anchor women on the local TV channel. She happened to be an attractive, fair-skinned, Black woman. One of the women was my supervisor, and represented the typical white, Southern aristocracy. She was particularly verbal about how beautiful and articulate this young Black woman was, and then proceeded to add, "I can't imagine her with a Black man." I stared at her with disbelief at what I had heard. I was also thankful that there were no Black staff within earshot. She was oblivious to the fact that her words were at all offensive. I removed myself from the circle and went to check on my patients. I was not equipped at the time to rebut her words, but as she later learned what my life was about, she avoided my company.

Another example of this aversion to racial intermixing regarding sexuality was much more covert and would have been denied had it been pointed out to well-meaning parents. Many young couples with young children came from the North to work with Voice of Calvary Ministries in Jackson, Mississippi. It seemed that when their children got to a certain age and began to notice the opposite sex, parents often moved on. While it was never admittedly stated by these parents that the possibility of inter-racial relationships forming was the motivation, this possibility was discussed as a probability among many of us. I also witnessed this in Lancaster, Pennsylvania in an urban, multi-racial church.

A lighter experience involved my late brother-in-law, Spencer. This event highlights the stereotype that some white folks have about the diminished intellectual ability of the Black male that is instead overshadowed by sexual virility and appetite. I went with my sister and Spencer to see the movie, *Amadeus*, which is about Mozart. The white employee selling the tickets looked at Spencer in surprise when he requested the tickets for *Amadeus* and asked him if he knew what the movie was about. Spencer assured him that he did. We laughed as he recounted the incident to us, but the ugly truth was not humorous. It revealed the prejudice against Black people having the intellectual capacity to appreciate a story of classical music and the persons who made it. There would not have been any questioning had we been buying tickets to a Spike Lee film, except for possibly why two white girls were going to see it.

I cannot ignore the irony that it was in Jackson, Mississippi that I would finally discover my own personal sexual revolution. Me, a little Mennonite girl, coming to the dark side of Mississippi to find greater illumination. There were several romantic conquests with those from my own clan, acceptable prospects that should have made me happy. It seemed that there was a restlessness in me with those who would provide a future much like the one I knew.

I began a relationship with a young man who first caught my eye as I gazed from the second-floor bathroom window of the Volunteer Service house where I lived. It overlooked a basketball court where the young men from the community came to play basketball. Brayton's physique and manner attracted me. He was a skilled basketball player and was fiercely competitive yet disciplined. He seemed to possess an aloofness that was demonstrated when he walked away from loud arguments or other verbal discourse from players. Plus, he was a gorgeous Black man. I was twenty-three, he was several years younger. And so, began the awakening of yearnings within me. A spark ignited the first time we kissed. I was intense, he was immature: what a combination. We defied all the barriers of society and hurt and healed one another. Our relationship lasted with intermittent break-ups and getting back together for the next five years.

During those break-ups there were other relationships. One of those was with a married man. What held me were his good looks, sensitivity, and intellect. While his marriage was on the rocks long before we met, I could not justify what I was doing. This relationship defied all the moral values I was raised with. Eventually I withdrew from the relationship when he declared his love for me, and I could not reciprocate. I kept imagining how I would feel if I was in his wife's position. I still had some principles!

I also came alive in other ways. I began to dress like I wanted and began to believe that I was beautiful and attractive to the opposite sex. I learned how to dance. Most weekends would find me at the roller-skating rink, disco skating to the rhythm of pulsating music, or couples skating to slow romantic songs. They say white girls don't have rhythm, but I developed rhythm and learned how to use it to my advantage. I rarely sat on the sidelines for couples' skates, and that felt good.

Brayton continued to be the love of my life. I was devastated yet understood when he enlisted in the Navy and was sent overseas. His father was a military man and the opportunities for young motivated Black men in Jackson, Mississippi were limited. He first declared his love for me from boot camp in a telephone call only having several minutes to say, "I love you, baby." My heart did somersaults. We continued to stay in touch, talking long hours on the phone sometimes in odd hours of the night depending where he was on the globe.

Our times together when he was on leave home grew more intense. We began to speak of marriage: what would work and what would not. However, I knew there were gaps in our relationship that time and love would never fill. I was growing up and maturing in what I needed in a relationship. On one of his leaves home we seemed to recognize the tenuousness of our future together. I also wanted to experience sexual expression in its totality and with someone I loved. While I had explored sexual expression in various other ways, I had never given myself completely. At the age of 27 I gave my virginity to Brayton. I shared myself with him, fully and without shame. I had waited 27 years to enter this physical realm of love. It was a conscious choice I made, not a careless act of the moment.

I was and will always be grateful for what Brayton taught me of love and of life. I learned the hurt of being Black in America, I learned the cost of loving someone of another race, and I learned the conflict of loving someone and facing the hurt as well as the joy in a relationship. We kept in touch on and off until I became engaged to another man. Brayton was my first love and my first lover, and I will never forget him.

    I did not defy the austere Mennonite/Evangelical regulations about sexual sins and the results thereof lightly. Several days later I visited my friend Gloria. Gloria was a young Black woman who had paid a price for becoming pregnant while not married. She was disciplined by the church we both attended by restricting her participation in her normal church activities. I went to see her to "confess" as it were what I had done. She listened intently. When I was finished, she seemed to be unsure of what I was looking for. "So did I do something wrong," I asked. She smiled and said, "Did you enjoy it?" I assured her I did. She replied, "That is what matters." I knew she was not encouraging an irresponsible "if it feels good do it" mentality. But rather she knew what it was to love someone and lose them and the desire to retain a part of that love. For her it was a child, for me a significant memory.

    Gloria was most likely judged by the church leadership as a poor role model to the children and young people she so effectively taught and influenced. Gloria held no animosity toward this regard but there would have been another way. What harm would have been done if she would have carried on her amazing ministry to children during her pregnancy? The discipline meted out to her was not for the benefit of the children who loved her and looked up to her, but for the need of church leadership to "make an example" of her "sin" and its consequences. I carried my secret close to my heart, sharing with those who would love and not judge my decision.

    I emerged a stronger woman, defeating the lies that wanted to hide my sexuality as a woman and warning about the sins of sexual pleasure. I learned that a woman's strength was her ability to consent or to not consent and the right to have that respected. I have no regrets about those years of exploration and development, and I believe that God was with me in it all.

I grew up with the idea that the ultimate success for a woman was to get married and have children. There was a negative stigma about "being an old maid." Just as I was coming to terms with the fact that I may be single for the rest of my life and feeling at peace with that idea, I met someone. It seemed like ill timing. I was going to finish my licensing exam for Registered Nursing and then climb aboard a Mercy ship or some other international adventure. But instead, this man walked into my life one Sunday morning at Voice of Calvary Fellowship. He was talking about South Africa and Apartheid, and what he and others were doing to change things.

There is a corny statement coined in reference to romantic relationships that says, "once you go Black, you never go back." There is something about the culture of African origin that calls to me. Perhaps it is the sense of community and "peopleness" in opposition to individuality, independence, and other determinants of success in mainstream, western mentality. This quality has consistently drawn me to communities and people of color.

Graham Cyster is a so called, "Coloured" South African. Coloured was a term given to mixed race individuals by the White Afrikaner government when it came to power in the late 1940s. Graham rejected this classification and continues to refer to himself as Black, as many progressive mixed-race individuals do. He has Asian Indian features resulting from his Malaysian genetic roots, with dark skin, dark eyes, and straight black hair. He also has some defining African features, full lips, and broad nose. He made it clear to me from the beginning that he was on his way back to his homeland after being in the U.S. and Great Britain intermittently for the past thirteen years. We met in January of 1985 and were married in January of 1986. I was 29, he was 37. The year in between was one of intense inner struggle, sorting out love from the grim realities of what life would be like in a racially divided and volatile South Africa. Added to the emotional challenges was resistance to our relationship from various sources that were surprising and painful.

Graham had been courting a particular branch of the Mennonite church to support the vision he had for a nonracial community and ministry in South Africa. He had initiated this relationship before we met and felt tremendous support and interest within the group. We attended a Mennonite conference in the Midwest where we were to meet with this group and solidify an arrangement for future involvement. After a couple of interactions, we felt the momentum cooling off. They diplomatically asked vague questions about our relationship in a public forum, and then pursued more pointed questions in private encounters with each of us individually.

I was approached by a retired missionary woman who remained single through her many years of service in Africa. She questioned me about my understanding of what Graham was called to do and what life would be like in South Africa. Her tone of questioning left no doubt in my mind that she disapproved of me, a white American, marrying an African man. I believe she assumed that I did not fit the mold for a missionary role based on my stylish appearance and confident bearing. Given that she only interacted with me individually for minutes before her gentle but pointed questioning, she had no idea of my life experiences that helped prepare me for where I was headed. Furthermore, she had one "African" experience which would not help her understand the context of South Africa, uniquely different than other African countries. I thanked her for her concern as we parted ways for other activities. Graham later shared with me that he was also questioned by the leadership about the wisdom of his decision to marry me. Consequently, we never received that promised support by the organization, however, various individuals stayed engaged with our work in South Africa.

Another, more troubling, encounter came from Trisha. She was someone I considered a friend and herself a person of color. We had known each other for years in Jackson. I had cared for her children, ate at her table, and attended church with her. One day, only months before I was due to be married, we happened to encounter each other at a community health clinic and she asked to speak to me privately. We went into one of the vacant offices where she emphatically expressed concerns and dismay that I was marrying Graham. She appeared angry as she raised questions about my ability to be anything but a hindrance to his ministry. She questioned, "what do you think you're doing, a white woman, going to racially charged South Africa, with a Black man?" I told her that I felt hurt by her accusations and thought she trusted me to be a standard for justice that could make a difference. She abruptly stated that she did not trust any white people. I left the encounter doubting myself and feeling deflated. I felt that I was being a target for her own anger at racial injustice, but that did not diminish the personal pain I felt from the interaction.

Even though the plans for my life with Graham together were pretty definite, I wanted to explore the truth. I wanted to know if there was even a bit of truth in her strong warnings. Fortunately for me, there was a gentleman named Thabo from Soweto, South Africa staying with a friend of mine for several weeks. Soweto is one of the largest Black South African townships and was a leader in the struggle for liberation in the 80s and 90s. I contacted him and asked him if I could come and speak to him. I went alone without Graham, as I believed this would afford Thabo the greatest freedom to speak into my life. After a few introductory pleasantries, I went straight to the heart of the matter and asked him if he thought I would be a hindrance to Graham's ministry. He listened carefully to my concerns and then laughed gently. Thabo emphatically supported our relationship, saying how our life together would be a witness to the fact that Black and white could love each other. He further stated that it would destroy myths and refute white dogma about people living together in harmony. My soul was lifted, and I felt a peace come over me. I could put this struggle to rest.

Somehow my relationship with Trisha survived but served as a stark reminder of how deep racial distrust goes. I do not remember having any conversation to resolve her strong feelings toward our marriage. However, she helped to organize events on our wedding day and in that way blessed us.

While the struggle within me was painful from these external forces, the struggle within myself from doubt, fear, and the unknown were excruciating at times. We were engaged only four months after we met. Graham proposed to me over the phone from South Africa! The total time we spent together in the same place added up to about four months in that year.

The rest of the time was long distance, hardly a normal courtship. Graham was in England defending his doctoral thesis at Kings College, in California in ministry, back in South Africa to prepare a place for us to live, and then back to Jackson, Mississippi. All the while I was preparing to take State Board Exams for Registered Nursing, working full time, and reading and seeing on TV what was happening in Apartheid South Africa. It was 1985 and the struggle was escalating, the young comrades (freedom fighters) could almost taste freedom and they were not going to back down. Bombs were going off; many countries applied political pressure and sanctions. The White Afrikaner government was feeling increased isolation and threat to its existence and in response, more repressive.

Amid all of this, my answer to Graham's marriage proposal was a yes. I loved and trusted this man. And I respected him. I knew he could keep up with me and better yet, he would give me the freedom to do what I needed to do to be all the woman God intended me to be. He was not intimidated by me. Having said that, I had questions that required my attention.

What was I doing? Was I crazy contemplating entering into this struggle? I knew that Graham was involved politically in the struggle for justice, so we were not going to be sitting on the safe sidelines. I was working the hospital night shift at the time. Some nights, in the wee hours of the morning, when everything was quiet, these questions made my gut wrench and panic rose in my throat. I knew my struggle was about more than who I should marry: it was about leaving all that was familiar and walking on water with little more than faith to sustain me. I had to process the thought that I could lose my life while engaging in the struggle. I was being called to look deep within myself and summon the very bedrock of the seed that God had planted there. Was it deep enough or strong enough to carry me into the heart of Apartheid South Africa?

Much of this struggle was done in solitude, with my God. It seemed it was too big for many to even contemplate with me. The reality was that for the eighteen months before I married Graham, I basically went underground socially as I worked almost full time as an LPN, while putting myself through Registered Nursing School. I had lived independently for so long from my parents and most of my older siblings and my journey was so different from theirs that it never occurred to me to reach out during this time of discernment.

I moved forward with plans to move to South Africa, giving away most of my possessions and boxing up the rest. I ended up with two footlockers of personal belongings that would be shipped ahead of me to my new home. Bit by bit a peaceful calm was taking hold of me, a surety that things were going to be alright, not easy, but alright. Graham and I spent hours in communication, discussing our future life together, addressing fears and misgivings, and balancing TV news with the reality that normal life happened amid chaos.

A few days before we were to exchange vows of eternal betrothal, I had an extremely difficult evening of turmoil. Graham and I were together. I expressed to him deep doubts about the future and my ability to bridge the vast chasm of change that was about to happen. He said gently to me that this was a struggle I needed to settle for myself. He could not help me. He knew then that if the future was going to work, it would have to be with my own certainty that this was the journey that I was being called to. I could see the pain in his eyes as he tenderly kissed me good night and said he would call me in the morning to see what I had decided.

I sat in the darkness for a few minutes, then knew I could not do this alone. I called my sister-in-law who was also one of my best friends. She and my brother had been in Jackson for several years, and we had grown close. I told her I needed to talk to someone desperately.

I remember standing outside her home in the dark as I relayed to her all my fears. With tears in my eyes, I confessed my doubts and feelings of inadequacy. I also felt a sense of shame doing this when everyone was making plans to attend the wedding, many with plans to travel from a distance.

I do not remember much of what she said, but I do remember a healing sense of acceptance and love from her, a love that accepted everything I was unloading without blame or judgement. As I cried on her shoulder with her arms around me, her acceptance of my weakness gave me strength. That night seemed to be a Gethsemane of sorts, and I needed one person to help me make it through. Having faced the very darkest of nights and survived, I was ready once again to greet the day with a renewed sense of strength.

Saturday, January 11, 1986, was our wedding. It was a simple ceremony conducted by my father. It included many of those who were involved in my life over the last seven years in Jackson. The marriage of a white Mennonite girl from rural Pennsylvania to a person of color from Cape Town, South Africa, in Jackson, Mississippi seemed illogical, but in many ways it made sense. Though very different in backgrounds, we had similar journeys that refined the values that drew us together. We both had shed many things that would have separated us and gained shared values of community, commitment to the poor, justice for the oppressed, and courage to work toward these ideals. We also had a shared faith.

At twenty-nine years of age, I left my country of birth, my family, and my close-knit church community. I entered a country halfway around the world that was entangled in a struggle for liberation. It was a gut-wrenching experience. Tears streaming down both our cheeks, my mother and I clung to each other until the last call for the flight to South Africa. We said our last goodbye and assured each other that we would both be okay. I crossed the ocean to the continent of Africa, sitting quietly beside my husband.

Dorcas with friends (front to back) Dorcas, Gloria, and Dessie.

Dorcas and Graham soon after their engagement (1985)

Dorcas and Graham's wedding in Jackson, Mississippi (January 11, 1986)

CHAPTER SEVEN

Living Illegally and Other Contraventions

No one could have fully prepared me for the challenges of life in South Africa. It was January of 1986. My relationship and covenant of marriage with Graham was a blatant provocation to pillars of Apartheid Law. We are an interracial couple, daring to live publicly as such in a country propped up by racist laws that determined every aspect of everyday life.

Graham is considered "coloured" by classification of South African law. He chooses to identify himself as Black in solidarity with the broader movement of progressive persons of color in South Africa. The South African Apartheid government, made up of white minority individuals, designated four categories of race. These were in order of privilege: white, coloured, Indian, and bantu (or Black). This identity was reflected in a mandatory "Identity Document" that persons of color were required to always carry on their person to be shown to white authorities on demand. The classification of racial groupings was designed to "divide and conquer" and prevent or destabilize any unity among persons of color, the majority population, that would threaten the grip of white minority rule. All persons of color were lumped together when it came to limiting access to public spaces, transportation, etc. The signage was clear: "Whites Only" to keep Black people out and "Non-Whites" so all would know their place.

The Immorality/Mixed Marriages Act was one of the first laws of Apartheid that originated in 1949 and one of the more draconian. This law prohibited sexual relations or marriage between non-white and white individuals. Even if the marriage took place in another country, it was not recognized as a legal marriage in South Africa. This oppressive law was invasive and personal, enforced by conducting police raids in homes and literally pulling couples apart in their beds. It was not repealed until June of 1985, six months before Graham and I were married. We proceeded with engagement and wedding plans with hopes that this change would happen prior to our move to South Africa. I firmly believe that the remnants of this law hampered the expediency of my Visa application. The delay had us both holding our breath while Graham reached out to influential contacts in South Africa to expedite the matter. My Visa arrived by courier a few days before our scheduled flight to Cape Town.

As our plane descended into Cape Town, anxious questions that I could not fully articulate overwhelmed me and swirled around in my head. What had I gotten myself into? I could feel the energy of my husband as he pointed out sights that were familiar to him, educating me to the disparities in housing that I was seeing.

At that time, all flights to Cape Town came across the Atlantic Ocean side of the continent, as South African airlines were banned from fly zones over most African countries in opposition to the Apartheid regime. This meant that my first view of my new homeland was of vast areas of sprawling

Townships, areas where Black and non-white individuals were relocated from prime space to make room for white residents. These areas were developed by government forces literally pushing non-whites toward the sea, away from city centers. Housing for Black people consisted of shacks, made of corrugated iron, crude lumber, black bags, or whatever was available and small concrete block cubicles. Most had no inside plumbing or adequate sewage provisions. These gave way to coloured housing, immense flats rising out of barren sand or small, one-story structures with minimal infrastructure. I later learned that these were the infamous Cape Flats, known for gang activity, extreme poverty, and crime. I would one day live in this community.

The Group Areas Act was another Apartheid law that challenged my marriage to Graham. While the Mixed Marriage Act was repealed to allow us to legally be married, the Group Areas Act prohibited us from living together. As a white person, I could not legally live or buy property in a designated non-white community, and my husband could not live or buy property in a designated white's only community. This law was still very much in the Constitution when we entered the country. Where and how were we to live?

Our initial welcome to Cape Town on that bright sunny day of summer (South Africa's seasons run conversely to America's: January is the heart of summer there) was enthusiastic and warm. It was my first time meeting Graham's family. As we descended the steps from the plane onto the tarmac at the airport, we were enthusiastically greeted by a loud, "there they are!" from one of my sisters-in-law. What followed was a jubilant and warm embrace from Graham's family. Kisses on the mouth and handshakes were the traditional greeting of a family member in the coloured community. I received the embraces from his parents, nine siblings, in-laws, and more than a dozen nieces and nephews and close family members with ease and appreciation. Graham later recounted that he had requested only a few family members be there to welcome us, forgetting that per cultural norms this would not have been acceptable. I was not nearly as overwhelmed as he protectively assumed I would be, and I relaxed into the atmosphere of acceptance and community. Everyone wanted to see and welcome into the family this white lady from across the seas with the strange American accent.

And so began the difficult journey of integrating into South African life. Several weeks later I applied for an Identity Document that classified me as white. This document afforded me permanent residence status in South Africa, and a driver's license. However, it could not solve the problem of how Graham and I were going to legally buy our home. We consulted a lawyer who had expertise in purchasing real estate with the condition of being married in "Community of Property." This provision entitled both husband and wife to have joint ownership of the property. He patiently listened to our situation and then had no answers for our dilemma. He said, "I need to consult with some of my colleagues and come back to you."

Several weeks later we had a follow up appointment. He seemed slightly nervous and unable to meet my eyes when he invited us into his office and motioned for us to sit down. Clearing his throat with a little cough, as he shuffled papers on his desk, he declared, "After consulting with colleagues and researching on my own, I have come up with a solution. The only currently viable way forward is to have you, Mrs. Cyster, sign an affidavit that states for the purpose of buying property you are a member of the coloured population group. Are you willing to do that?" Without hesitation I stated that I was fine with that. The attorney appeared visibly relaxed, sitting back in his chair after pushing the paperwork in my direction for my signature. We left his office minutes later.

As I got on the elevator to return to street level and leave, I asked myself what kind of a system was this that asked me to commit perjury to meet their petty specifications. This white lawyer was one of the more progressive ones, and this was his best option, given the law of the land. I then smiled to myself, secure in the fact that my identity did not rest on South African dictates. In a country of prescribed identity, mine was strong.

We purchased a simple little house in a coloured jurisdiction. The community was welcoming. My neighbor coached me in our shared pregnancy experience, my first child, her fifth. She became a true friend in supporting me through pregnancy symptoms, advising me what to take for nausea and other complaints. We had tea together and discussed our husbands. We laughed together. Our Muslim neighbors invited us to their religious celebrations. Their little girl appeared at our door, puppy in arms, offering it to me when our dog got stolen. Our dog did come back weeks later after escaping the clutches of those who had stolen her, bruised and thin, but alive! Life was good.

Within weeks I had put the finishing touches on our home, learned to drive on the other side of the road, and navigated grocery shopping. I began to learn about the sociological extremes between Black and white realities, and the complex balancing act of those in between. The coloured population in Cape Town represents the largest collection of this grouping in the country. They enjoyed the advantages of not being Black, yet there were constant reminders in political and societal laws that they were far less than white. Graham's family and many other coloured individuals lived within these parameters. This framework provided a precarious stability for keeping their family safe and surviving the daily challenges of life.

Graham and I were and are activists at heart. We chose to identify with the struggle for justice and liberation of all people in South Africa. For us that meant getting involved with the poorest of the poor, the most disenfranchised; in South Africa, that was the Black communities. For me that meant utilizing my nursing skills while drawing on what I learned from my experiences in the racially divided American South.

Before leaving the U.S., I had successfully completed my RN training and passed the National Exam for Licensure as a Registered Nurse. When I got to SA, I discovered that my RN License did not meet the criteria of the South African RN Licensure. I pursued obtaining additional requirements to qualify, however, while educating myself to South African hospital policy for Nursing, I discovered some disturbing information. Apartheid inequalities existed in pay and staffing policy for nurses. There were gradients of pay rates depending on racial classification. There were segregated wards within the hospitals, and they were staffed accordingly. I had already decided that I wanted to work in an underserved area in the Black Townships, but also wanted to get licensed. As I sorted through the South African Nursing Board's rejection of my hard-earned U.S. license and considered what would be personal ethical barriers working within the South African Nursing field, I decided to forgo licensing in South Africa. I informed the SA Nursing Board of my decision to not move ahead in this regard, and that I would be working at a non-government clinic in a Black Township.

The clinic where I volunteered was Crossroads Clinic. It was developed by a white South African doctor. He was an activist who refused to do required military service due to the role the military played in oppressive and violent actions against Black people. Along with other progressive medical professionals, he started a clinic in a shack community with no medical resources. It was funded independently by donations from overseas and professionals that donated their time or worked for minimal wages. Graham had a relationship with the founding doctor and had explored the possibility of my involvement there. At that time, all municipal health clinics were provided and funded by the SA government. They controlled the access and quality of health care. Both aspects of these clinics were determined by what population group was served. Clinics in white areas were much more accessible and better resourced than those in non-white areas.

The nursing authority's only response was that I could not collect wages as a nurse. I had already intended to volunteer my time, so this was not a barrier. I suspect the nursing authority was a bit surprised at my decision to practice in this capacity as a white person.

My days were filled with contrasts and contradictions. I was living in a relatively middle-class coloured community and practicing third-world medicine at Crossroads Clinic. Crossroads was a squatter community, never intended for housing, and bulldozed multiple times by the South African government troops. Crossroads was where I encountered South African nursing practice in the raw. White-owned mining companies and other corporations required cheap labor, which was to be found in the rural areas where Black families traditionally lived. They wanted the men to come to provide the labor, but never intended the families to follow. Same sex hostels that resembled primitive barracks were built by the South African government to accommodate the families that followed the workers. This was an untenable arrangement. It not only fractured families but eroded the possibility of economic stability for the Black community. As a result, informal settlements sprang up as courageous women migrated to the cities where their husbands lived. Crossroads was the largest informal settlement in Cape Town. Over the years it had become notorious for extreme poverty, primitive living conditions, and the relentless efforts of the South African government to destroy it. In the middle of this settlement was the clinic where I worked for almost two years.

My decision to work in such a volatile situation confused and somewhat disturbed Graham's family. Their goal was to keep me safe and protect me from all the logistics of protest, violence, and danger. This was the way most coloured individuals lived their lives, in the safety of their coloured bubble. Many thought that Black people were below them, not only economically but intellectually. Coloured people had no reason to cross the racial divide that afforded them more privilege, even as they themselves were oppressed by a white unjust system.

Graham broke out of this norm as he pursued education and opened his mind to progressive movements within South Africa. As a youth his family tried to contain and prohibit his inquiring mind. I am sure they were relieved when he chose to go into ministry, thinking it would quell his thirst for liberation and equality. I am sure they thought he would settle down when he came back to South Africa with a wife to set up a home. Instead, not only had his desire for political liberation for the oppressed been fueled and refined, but he came back with a woman who was an activist in her own right!

My mother-in-law tried to put me in touch with persons who could possibly provide me with a more respectable place of work. They had difficulty understanding why Graham and I would want to be involved in the Black townships. Coloured folks did not go to the townships, they did not interact with Black people except as day laborers or domestic help.

Ah yes, domestic help. We had only been living in our house for a few weeks when there was a knock at the door. It was a Black woman wanting to know if we had work for her. I was dumbfounded. What work would I delegate to her? I was planning to clean the house, wash our clothes, do our dishes, etc. I had no need for help, especially as a white woman having a Black woman do my dirty work. I had come from the American South where I saw Black nannies in palatial white suburbs waiting for the bus at the end of the day to take them to overcrowded, urban communities. Why would I perpetuate such a colonial mentality?

As the woman waited outside, my husband patiently explained to me that to give her work and pay her well was her survival. It would mean food for her family. I reluctantly agreed yet it was so painful to me to have her come weekly to clean our house. The only consolation was that we paid her more than double what she would have been paid by others doing the same work. My life was daily filled with opportunities to broaden my understanding and yet remain firm in my convictions about justice.

One aspect of our early life together as a mixed-race couple that repeatedly surprised me was the attention we received in public life. Stares of disbelief and finger pointing was a regular occurrence as we did our grocery shopping or other routine activities. This attention came from coloured and white folks, rarely, if ever, from Black folks. Black folks tended not to see as much distinction between white and coloured South Africans as both racial groupings were regarded higher than theirs. Also, as in my experiences with those marginalized at the "bottom" of society, they know what it is to be isolated and demonstrate the true quality of Ubuntu that includes acceptance of all. I could understand somewhat from white folks who regarded anything less than white unacceptable for sexual relations and marriage. But what was hard for me to understand was coloured individuals finding Graham and me together unusual. I would ask Graham, "don't they know how they got here? Somewhere in the last 40 years they had a white, Black, or whatever mixture in their family." He would just shake his head and smile.

Mostly I ignored the attention, but sometimes it was irritating and uncomfortable. Mixed marriages and the emergence of families in public were extremely rare in our first years of married life. As restrictive laws were abolished, more interracial relationships emerged especially between white and coloured individuals. Marriages that crossed into Black African communities were almost nonexistent in the 80s. Looking back, I understand how effectively Apartheid influenced people's psyche and affected rational thinking, but at the time I only knew it was one more thing to get used to.

I hovered between emotions of anger and hope within this land of incredible beauty and wealth and yet abject poverty and oppression. There were so many contradictions and questions without answers. In the American South where I had lived for almost seven years, there was a social apartheid and I had gotten used to breaking down those barriers. In South Africa, there was a whole legal system that enforced Apartheid as a way of life. It was the extreme of anything I had previously encountered. Amid adjusting to the many changes and making life work, I experienced times of deep grief and loneliness.

During the day, I was "strong" and "courageous," as others described me. At night, after kissing my husband goodnight, I often turned toward the wall and wept.

I wept for the oppression and raw poverty around me. I wept for the disparity and the blissful unknowing of the privileged. I wept for the loss of my community and friends in Jackson, Mississippi who would understand and weep with me. I wept for the loss of all that was familiar, components of life that worked for me and felt safe. I wept for the loss of my family, now oceans away. I wept because once again I stood out, in a strange land, with a brown husband, speaking a different type of English, alone and isolated. I wept for the finality of my new life in South Africa, not a one-to-three-year mission assignment, but a move. South Africa was the place where I would start a family. South Africa was home.

One Sunday at church, a few weeks before leaving the states, we sang one of my favorite songs. I closed my eyes as I sang the last verse of "Pass Me Not, O Gentle Savior." It was if I had a prophetic moment. I envisioned myself in South Africa, alone, recounting this scene and claiming these words:

> Thou the spring of all my comfort, more than life to me,
> Whom have I on earth beside Thee?
> Whom in heav'n but Thee?
> Savior, Savior, hear my humble cry;
> While on others Thou are calling, Do not pass me by.

How could I have possibly known that I would feel such aloneness and grief? I believe it was one of those moments of grace, that would later provide a comforting touchpoint to the familiar. These experiences of grief and loss were necessary to gradually let go of the old and embrace the new. Finally, I accepted that home could be anywhere my heart was. My heart was in South Africa, where together, with my husband, our life had meaning and a common purpose.

First racial segregation sign that Dorcas saw at a beautiful, white sandy beach outside of Cape Town, South Africa (1986), signifying Whites Only

Informal housing in Khayelitsha, Cape Town's largest Black Township.

CHAPTER EIGHT

This is Not My War

All was not well as we rounded the bend. I was traveling with my friend who was a doctor to Crossroads Clinic where I had been working for the past several months. It was early morning, and we should have smelled the smoke of primer stoves as families cooked breakfast and prepared for the day. Instead, we saw women with children sitting along the road on bags of belongings, noticeably displaced. Where there were once rows of uneven shacks made of corrugated iron and wood, smoldering rubble lay. Beyond the charred areas, black smoke and large flames were rising amidst the chaos of gun shots and men running with clubs and other crude weapons. We realized we were now in an active war zone and had no idea what we would find at the clinic or even if it was still standing.

It was June of 1986; I had been in South Africa less than a year and the whole country was in a low-grade civil war. Pockets of resistance escalated throughout the country as Freedom Fighters (labeled terrorists by the South African government) renewed their commitment to liberation for all. As a result, the South African Defense Force (SADF) equally renewed their efforts to maintain control by declaring a state of emergency. This measure allowed detention and torture of any suspected "terrorist" without a trial.

The African National Congress (ANC) was the government in exile, led by Nelson Mandela. Nelson Mandela was still incarcerated after a pseudo trial that sentenced him to life in prison for treason. As a skilled lawyer, now rotting in the maximum-security prison on Robbin Island, he maintained leadership of the struggle for liberation. The ANC was a banned organization by the South African government. The leaders were either imprisoned or exiled to surrounding countries. The ANC trained Comrades, the foot soldiers for the struggle, in secluded camps. They were then sent covertly back into the country to lead maneuvers to overthrow the repressive and illegitimate South African government.

Crossroads was a hotbed for conflict between the young, progressive Comrades and a group of older, less politicized, residents known as "Witdoeke" (Afrikaans for White Band). The Witdoeke became puppets of the SADF and were compensated with alcohol and money for their allegiance to maintaining the repressive status quo. The SADF instructed them to wear white bands on their arms to identify themselves. They waged war on the Comrades and served as informers to the SADF in identifying the resistance leaders and anticipated actions. The South African soldiers would know who to cover and assist in the struggle by the white arm bands. This strategy by the South African Government was employed throughout the country and served as "proof" of "Black on Black violence." The government-controlled news spread this propaganda internally and internationally to gain support for increased repressive measures.

The Crossroads Clinic stood as a bastion of hope for the people of Crossroads. Here was a space where white and Black people worked together and encouraged free thought and liberation. The clinic was staffed by a mixture of white, coloured, and Black doctors, nurses, and support staff. It was a safe space for progressive political discussions and to hold community meetings. On any given day, you could hear Black African patients singing hymns in four-part harmony lined up on backless benches waiting to be seen for treatment. The founding doctor of the clinic was on the South African government's watch list due to his political views and international connections.

This clinic was part of the progressive movement for justice, and Graham was acquainted with the founding doctor. It is through their relationship that I became involved with the clinic and thus entered into health care as a form of political resistance. The clinic was a nemesis to the South African government as it was funded by international finances and provided a humanitarian service, yet according to them, it fostered "radical ideas" and supported "Communists." As I travelled to the clinic with my doctor friend on that tragic day, we hoped that the community had protected the clinic and that the SADF respected this space as a neutral place of healing.

The clinic was intact. It was standing strangely alone while most of the surrounding dwellings had been torched by the Witdoeke with the assistance of the SADF. The area was largely controlled by SADF military vehicles and armed soldiers. We grouped with the other medical staff to decide what to do. We knew there were other areas nearby where skirmishes were still happening, and Comrades were being injured. Injured Comrades, needing treatment, would be afraid to go into the local hospitals for fear of being arrested and detained. We decided to split up and look for those who may need treatment at other sites. A doctor asked me to stay with some of the wounded at the clinic.

As the doctor led me into the treatment room that served as a temporary triage space, I noticed that all the men wore the white arm bands. I was surrounded by Witdoeke, people who were against all that I and the clinic stood for. The doctor asked me to assist a man lying on a stretcher who had a compound fracture in his lower leg. Here I was, a white woman, surrounded by stern-faced Black men, worn from battle, eyeing me suspiciously as I rendered support to their fellow soldier.

I clicked into nurse mode and looked at the exposed gunshot wound that had fractured the bone. There was no splint to be found, so my job was to use my hands to form a temporary splint to keep the bone from breaking through the skin. As I stood there listening to the injured man's moans while his blood oozed through my fingers, my initial thoughts were not for my own safety but the tragedy of the situation. I looked around the room at the men surrounding me. They sat with bandaged wounds and primitive weapons beside them, battle worn, eyes averted. I felt compassion for them even as they had betrayed their own people. They too, were part of a manipulative government strategy that attempted to continually divide people in order to maintain power and control. I provided support until an ambulance took my patient to the hospital. He would be safe there, unlike the Comrades, as he was aiding the SADF.

The rest of the day I went with others to multiple temporary treatment sites where the injured needed help. I visited feeding stations for the many who found themselves homeless from the mass burning of homes. Muslim groups had quickly set up portable cooking facilities where soup and bread were being served. Side by side we worked in this humanitarian crisis. Always, at the perimeters of the area, giant armed military vehicles called Casspirs were patrolling. Fresh-faced white boys, some barely out of their teens, carrying large guns rode on top of the Casspirs. They were too young to realize the enormity of what they were a part of. They had driven back the resistance it seemed, but that was just for today and they did not begin to comprehend that nothing could stop this movement toward freedom.

Later that evening I returned home. As I entered our home, Graham greeted me with relief and great emotion. He informed me that he was aware of what was happening in Crossroads and had attempted to find me. Unable to locate me, he had returned home to cook a pot of food for us when I finally did return. Cooking for him was therapeutic, a way to do something for my return and not to think the worst. As we hugged each other long and close, my mind was distracted. Part of me was still with those who would be homeless tonight with no warm bed…some having lost loved ones, or not knowing if they were safe…the little children, afraid and not understanding.

Where did I fit into all of this? This was not my war… or was it? Was this just the struggle within the borders of South Africa or was this part of a global struggle? Why did I get to come home to a safe community? How could I just act normal and engage with those around me who did not know or want to know that there was a war going on just miles down the road? Did they not wonder about the grey smoke on the horizon? Did they not want to know that there were fellow South Africans living each day in hell?

This *was* my war. My country America had propped up the system of Apartheid for years in South Africa by refusing to call it out. They refused to apply economic sanctions as requested by leaders of the South African liberation struggle, which would have crippled the power of the South African government. Instead, the United States joined with other European countries in "constructive engagement," an arrangement that allowed these countries to benefit from South African mineral wealth while still appearing to be doing something about the oppression of Black people. America still had Nelson Mandela on their "Terrorist List." It was befitting for me to find myself in this small primitive clinic room, literally holding together the wounds of injustice that I had benefitted and unknowingly contributed to.

I was part of a global phenomenon: the struggle between the rich and powerful and the poor and disenfranchised, the attempt to preserve comfort and privilege over sharing the God-given right to live in a democratic and just society. Now, here was my time to cross over and help right some of the wrong. I could not isolate myself or participate in the convenient blindness of groups with more privilege in South Africa. My passion was strong to carry on the fight. I would serve with those who led this struggle and in other struggles wherever I may find myself. I knew there were risks: I had faced that possibility before I ever left the shores of America.

Before I went to South Africa with Graham, I had many conversations with him about the risks of going to South Africa during these volatile years. I had to have my own times of doubt and reckoning with my Creator about life and death.

I loved living, but I could not stop living and doing what I was called to do if I did not consider how I felt about death. I had to believe that there was a power greater than myself that held my ultimate well-being in hand and that faith and wisdom would guide me.

I had only been in South Africa for several months prior to the chaos in Crossroads. It was in a sense a baptism by fire, an awakening to what I was up against. I continued to work with Crossroads Clinic. The situation got more volatile and the SADF police presence was more intense. They were intent on restricting white people access to Crossroads and other Black Townships to prevent eyewitnesses to the brutality they used to restore law and order. They set up military roadblocks at major roads leading to Crossroads. We met as clinic staff to decide how to move forward. One of the doctors had connections in higher places who got us a copy of a letter with the required official seal that we could use to get through the roadblocks. We duplicated the letter and put our names in the blank spaces in case it was needed as proof that we had government approval to enter Crossroads. I learned that sometimes unjust laws and restrictions needed to be broken for the greater calling to justice.

Working at Crossroads Clinic was a privilege and a humbling learning experience. I was a white American, unable to speak the main African Language (isiXhosa) in Cape Town. I dressed in a very Western style and knew so little of the culture when I arrived. Again, I had a choice to largely interact with the English-speaking doctors or be a quiet presence with my peers who were Black African nurses. I chose to do the latter.

My main mentor in the "treatment room" where I was assigned to work was the equivalent of an American Licensed

Practical Nurse. She spoke little English but was not afraid to try it out on me. She showed me how to suture cuts and clean and treat burns. As the RN working there, I got the task of administering massive doses of antibiotics to those with sexually transmitted infections and intravenous medications for chronic diseases.

At teatime, which was religiously maintained, I sat quietly with my peers. They spoke their mother tongue, and I sat and listened. I believe they had never witnessed a white person quite like me content to respect their leadership and direction with humility and grace. It was many years later that I was introduced to the term "cultural humility." Unknowingly, I was modelling this concept which I learned out of extensive intentional behavior as a white person of privilege in relating to individuals who experienced discrimination, repression, and hate. It is a discipline that comes from consistent examining of one's own racism and bias that mitigates against the ability to remain silent and learn from those different than you. Yes, remain silent even when you think you know better!

I would like to believe that my attitude formed a strong foundation for the development of a new model of delivering health care. As the clinic staff regrouped after the destruction of much of Crossroads, we discussed the development of a new model of care. Through careful listening to clinic staff from the community, it became apparent that more broad-based accessible care with a focus on prevention was needed, with treatment secondary.

We worked together as clinic staff to develop a Community Health Worker project. This method of care would empower individuals selected by the community to be trained in teaching healthy habits to prevent disease, provide basic first aid skills, and treatment of chronic conditions. These Community Health Workers (CHWs) would be given supplies and on-going training to meet the basic health care needs of the community. The CHWs spoke the language of the people and personally knew the struggles of the community. They met regularly with the professional clinic staff for case review and on-going education. I assisted with this project until my swelling abdomen made navigating the primitive clinic conditions difficult. I was pregnant with our first child. Observing my pregnancy brought smiles to my patients and co-workers and for a moment we shared a common human experience amid vastly different lives.

I did not return to my work at Crossroads Clinic after giving birth. The demands of new parenting in a foreign country required all my energy and time. Frontline political resistance now took on different consequences if something should happen to me, now parenting a newborn. The old clinic was ultimately flattened as was the entire Crossroads area. It seemed there was little energy to completely rebuild after the massive destruction of homes. The new model of utilizing Community Health Workers with old shipping containers as satellite sites for the clinic supported the community for several years. A new clinic was built at a strategic site and continued to deliver critical health care services to adjoining Black Townships who did not have accessible care. Government health care expanded when a democratic government took over in 1994 with the goal to deliver equitable health care for all.

Dorcas with Crossroads Clinic ambulance. The clinic staff requested she park it at her house as she was new to the country and not being watched by the Security Police.

Dorcas assisting at the Islamic first aid clinic set up during the Crossroads conflict. Note the smoke in the background from the homes destroyed.

Informal housing built with corrugated iron and wood.

CHAPTER NINE

American Citizen Born Abroad

My innocent childhood plans of having lots of kids and living on a farm had receded years before as I ventured into the world and experienced life in all its beauty and ugliness. The years in America's Deep South and now in Apartheid South Africa made me question why people would bring pure, unspoiled beings from heaven into a world fraught with racism, violence, and incivility.

In the first year since I had moved to Cape Town in 1986, I was awed by the natural beauty of my husband's motherland. I was also deeply moved and repelled by the horrific system that oppressed millions of Black African people while enabling the repressive white Afrikaner government to provide opulent lifestyles for white people. I had personally experienced the segregated government policies that divided people on skin coloring alone. I as a white person was prohibited from buying a house with my husband who was mixed race or "coloured" as categorized by the South African government. I witnessed the brutal repression each week as I entered the Black Townships to do nursing. Yet anything I experienced paled in comparison to the daily impact that this system forced on the non-white masses. It prescribed where they lived and worked, where their children went to school, what beaches they swam in, where on the train they rode, what hospital they went to…. the list went on.

Since then, I had given much thought to the idea of having children. Having experienced the environment of the country that was now my home, I was deeply conflicted. My husband and our South African family were extremely excited about the possibility of a child and saw it as a natural progression in the circle of life. I did not consciously decide I would never give birth, but unconsciously put it way back there in my mind, and it kept getting pushed back further as I witnessed the challenges that lay ahead not only for me but also for a child of color in South Africa.

Amid this mental dialogue with God and myself, I had an experience that gave me hope and brought perspective to my fears. I was honored to experience a holy moment in a corrugated iron shack erected on the vast sandy wasteland known as Crossroads where I was working as a nurse. Each day when coming to work, I was disturbed by the large armed vehicles known as Caspirs patrolling the squatter community. Seven or eight young white men with guns ready protruded from the top of each of these pre-historic looking vehicles. They were "protecting" the rest of the country from the Black people who carried water vessels on their heads, built their cooking fires, and watched their children running around playing with sticks and old tires.

One day during my regular duties of suturing, cleaning burns, injections, and bandaging, I was called to go with one of the doctors who was urgently beckoned by one of the community residents. The woman indicated that her daughter was in labor and there was no time to call an ambulance to take her to a local birthing center. There was no time for thought or to make excuses that I had little experience with the birthing process, never even having had a child myself. I went.

Following close behind the doctor, we walked hurriedly through narrow paths in the sand, through a maze of shacks, along fences made of sticks, being careful not to trip over the occasional thin, scavenging dog or the numerous scantily clad toddlers. Finally, we reached the shack where the woman was in labor.

As we entered, I noted the extended family women were all in attendance and greeted us with urgency and expectancy. They busied themselves in the first room, boiling water, making food, and caring for children. The next room was a makeshift "birthing room." The floor was lined with newspaper and the minimal furniture was moved to the side. A naked woman was squatting on the floor, moaning softly while another woman supported her. It was obvious the delivery was imminent.

I stood close, yet cautiously remote; drawn to the scene, yet anxiously distant. I felt my lack of experience professionally and was not sure what I would be required to do. The doctor bent down and spoke to the woman; she seemed to know what to do and really did not need our intervention. We were there to assist if the natural process required it. However, in what seemed like only moments, the brown bundle of new life was thrust from the woman's loins with a gush of life-supporting water and blood. The newborn's umbilical cord was clamped and cut. The doctor instinctively handed the newborn to me as the attending health care worker. I stepped forward, reflexively reaching out to cradle the baby boy as he was handed to me in a wrapping of newspaper.

Then I had a holy moment I will never forget. As my arms felt the heavy warmth and moisture of the womb through the newsprint paper, my eyes became riveted on this wriggling, vibrant new life. A barrage of questions crowded my mind: Why did this woman feel it was worth bringing a baby into this life? What was his future? Would he grow up with anger toward his oppression? Would he even grow up?

The moments I held this infant seemed like an eternity of paradoxes.... yet as I handed him over to the loving arms of the caregivers, I saw none of my confusion in their eyes. They began to sing and welcome this new member of the family, and soon the whole community rejoiced with them, the singing reverberated down the sandy pathways, the children picked up the joy and giggled, the tired laborers returning from work, smiled. It travelled to the perimeter of the shacks and echoed softly to the armed soldiers in the Caspirs, and I am sure they wondered like me: how could there be joy amidst this squalor?

As I made my way back to the clinic and later back home, a transformation was happening in me that would forever shape my way of doing life. This mother knew something that I did not know; she knew that as long as there was life, there was hope that things could get better. Maybe not in her lifetime but surely in her new son's lifetime, freedom would come. To stand still and do nothing was certain death of that hope. She knew that each new day was a gift from God and was there to be lived to its fullest potential, regardless of the outcome. She was a lesson in living for the moment, as tomorrow her house may be destroyed, and she would once more have to begin again.

I was late in getting my period. I was experiencing strange reactions to various smells, and I was suddenly out of breath while doing the aerobics class that I had been doing for months. When I relayed this to one of the doctors I worked with, she produced a pregnancy test with instructions to take it.

Now, for me as I peed on the pregnancy test stick, it was crunch time. The pink plus mark on the pregnancy test brought an abrupt end to my abstract thoughts of denial that floated out there in the "I'll think about it later" zone. It was time to come to terms with the cells of new life that were growing within me. Bringing new life into the world most often brings a reorganizing, a rethinking of the future, but the context for me was particularly daunting.

I was in Cape Town, South Africa. My family of origin was oceans away. My medical familiarity was in the context of American hospitals where I had trained as a Registered Nurse, and I had conceived this child with a South African man committed to the struggle for liberation in a country in political turmoil!

And so….as I looked at the dark pink positive sign of pregnancy, I cautiously embraced a feeling of expectancy. Not without some fear of the unknown, but I knew that others had gone before me. They had faced the dark clouds on the horizon, and they had weathered the storms with greater odds than mine, emerging stronger and more determined than before to embrace life and the continuance of it. I decided that I would carry this new life with courage and determination that within me lay the potential to make her world a better place, and to live in the freedom of all that she was intended to be.

Even before she entered the world, our baby's pending arrival brought challenges to the Apartheid system. Inter-racial relationships were unheard of and illegal just two years prior, so couples bringing mixed-race infants into this unchartered territory was a new experience. The obstetrician who provided my prenatal care was white, and Graham and I had open dialogue with him at our first appointment. We inquired how he felt about our relationship and delivering our baby. Without hesitation he assured us that he welcomed us into his practice and into his capable medical hands. He said, "I would like to apologize on behalf of all white South Africans who support and perpetuate this system of segregation. I believe God sees us all as equal." He even prayed with us, asking God's blessing on the health and delivery of our unborn baby. Dr. Shelton was an active member of the Anglican Church of South Africa, a denomination known for more progressive thinking and social action, the denomination of Reverend Desmond Tutu, Archbishop. It was just what we needed to feel that we were in safe and competent hands.

Many months later when our baby girl refused to leave the warm, safe, haven that was her home for 9-plus months, we were instructed to go immediately to the hospital for an induction of labor. The maternity hospital in which I was to give birth was segregated, which I was not aware of. As individuals were admitted for care it was decided based on the race of the mother where they were to go. Graham had dropped me off at the main entrance and went to park the car.

The hospital staff must have gotten instructions from the doctor to start the induction without delay, so I was soon taken to a ward where the vaginal suppository would be inserted that would get my labor started. However, minutes later before they even administered the medication, my husband appeared on the floor. I immediately noted the hushed confusion and discussion among the nurses. Soon they rushed me into a private room, escorted my husband in, and closed the door. Graham informed me what was going on. I had not paid any attention to the fact that all the women in the ward where the inductions were happening were white. My mind, totally focused on the birth of our daughter, could not even comprehend the dilemma I inadvertently caused, nor did I care. I was a white woman giving birth with a Black, mixed-race partner who had every intention of being involved in the process in a segregated hospital.

Several minutes passed, then several more. No one came to administer the medication to induce my labor as was ordered by our doctor. Graham was getting agitated. I was assuring him that everything was alright with our baby and to prove it I reached above my bed and found a stethoscope. Putting it on my abdomen, I located the strong, rapid, reassuring heartbeat of our little one. I smiled. He smiled as well, but then said, "I am going to go outside and see what is happening, if I need to threaten the press or other means to get prompt attention, I will." I knew there was no stopping him. Whatever he said motivated one of the nurses to promptly attend to my needs. We were then taken to another private room for the duration of my labor.

The doctor soon arrived, and I have no idea whether the nurses were white or people of color who assisted the doc in bringing my healthy, baby girl into the world. To even consider the importance of this is incongruous to me. I only know my first conscious thought when back on the ward waiting for my baby to be brought to me, was *so I guess it was safe to put me on a white floor. The other white mamas would not be traumatized by a Black man.* To be fair, it was apparent to me that the majority of the white women did not seem distressed in any way with our presence for the next several days until we were discharged to home. The impetus seemed to be from the staff and administration attempting to maintain the law of the land while facing the realities of change in the country.

Elena Ruth Cyster was born on April 27, 1987. Elena was registered with the American Consulate's Office in Cape Town as "An American Citizen Born Abroad." This provided her with American citizenship and the ability to have an American passport. She would be able also to have South African citizenship one day if she so desired. She also needed to have a full South African birth certificate. Ah yes, another challenge.

When I went to file for the birth certificate, I was required to put what race I wanted the child to be classified as. I asked the registrar what I was to fill in as my baby had a white American mother and a mixed-race South African father. I genuinely did not know what to put. She looked uncomfortable and then consulted a reference document. Returning to face me she said because she has a "coloured" father, she needs to be classified as coloured. I obediently filled in the space as I was told. Again, the legal identity of my child had less significance to me than to those who were enforcing the laws of Apartheid. I would fight for her no matter what and do everything in my power to have her not be defined by a prescribed identity.

We now had an American passport for our baby girl and were on our way to do fund raising ministry in England and then to visit family in the U.S. We went through check-in at the D.F. Malan Airport, which was renamed Cape Town International Airport in 2018; D.F. Malan was one of the prime architects of Apartheid.

The airport security staff blatantly stared at us. Here we were in 1987, most of the Apartheid laws still in place, a white woman and a man of color: what would the baby look like was most likely a question in their minds. As I noted a young white security woman gazing intently at our three-month-old baby girl and then whispering to her colleague, I suddenly had enough! Many times I had ignored the stares and the ignorance, but today was not going to be one of them! I think I was emboldened by the excitement of travel to places where I knew there would be no stares, only love and acceptance.

I stopped and looked her directly in the face, with my beautiful, olive-skinned baby with big dark eyes perched on my hip, and said "Yes, she is our child, from my mixed-race husband and me, a white woman, and see she does not have spots or stripes, isn't she beautiful?" The white security woman immediately averted her eyes and flushed red and waved us through. My husband just smiled and gently shook his head. I felt good, as I was certain the security woman would remember this day as a day she was educated to the changes that were happening in her country, the beliefs she was raised with challenged and exposed in an uncomfortable encounter.

Elena has memories of segregated swimming areas prohibited to her in her early childhood. But she also has memories of having all the benefits of getting to know individuals of all races, religions, and cultures. She was one year old when we moved into an inter-racial lifestyle community. She shared life every day with children and adults of every shade of Black, brown, and white. She was exposed to people living in great poverty and learned the importance of sharing food, clothing, toys, and resources necessary for life. She witnessed and experienced situations that many children will never face, including interaction with security forces because of the work that her father did, unaware of the magnitude of that interaction.

Today she remembers a secure childhood for the most part. Even though toys were sparse by American standards, she remembers open spaces to run and animals to enjoy. She was loved by families on both sides of the ocean. Elena's birthday, April 27th became Freedom Day in South Africa in 1994 when Nelson Mandela was elected president in the first democratic election.

Elena was ten years old when we moved to America. The culture shock and feelings of isolation as an immigrant in an American family with Western values and integrating into a white community were often painful. But that is her story to tell. The seeds of justice and compassion for others motivate her current practice as a mental health therapist. She is married to a man who has risen to the challenge of learning all that he can about South Africa and the struggle for justice around the world. She has given us a wonderful granddaughter.

CHAPTER TEN

Mama's Little Hope

My parents were crossing the Atlantic and coming to visit! It was December of 1989 and another new life was growing inside of me. Months earlier Graham and I had planned this child. In anticipation of my parents' visit, we calculated when best to become pregnant. I wanted to be past the first few months when I experienced nausea and yet not too close to my due date as to be too cumbersome for the adventures we had planned. I was due to give birth in February of 1990, which had me in my early third trimester when they arrived. This child was anticipated with excitement and cautious optimism that South Africa was headed for a better place.

South Africa was under increased pressure from the U.S., Great Britain, and other countries to dismantle Apartheid, release Nelson Mandela, and begin taking steps to a democratic government. While glimpses of hope were on the horizon, fear of reprisal from many white people precipitated an anxiety of uncertainty. The oppressed people's thirst for liberation was palpable, and the tension was mounting.

My parents arrived just before Christmas. December and January are a time of vacation and holiday in SA as it is the beautiful days of summer. Christmas is often spent at the beach as it is in the Southern Hemisphere where seasons are opposite from North America. We planned activities to do with them throughout the month they were with us. One of the trips we planned was coordinated with a conference for Mennonite North American missionaries that was held in Lesotho. Lesotho is a small land-locked independent country within the borders of South Africa. While we were never missionaries supported and governed by North American church boards, we partnered at times with their activities.

One afternoon was dedicated to recreation, and the organizers presented various options. My parents chose to visit a site where local artisans made pottery and other items that were then taken to the U.S. for sale in return for fair profits back to the artisans. Graham and I along with Elena who was two years old at the time chose to do a mountain excursion riding horseback. It was led by experienced Basotho (the term used for Lesotho identity) men and the horses were Basotho ponies, known for their steadiness and ability to carry riders safely across the rocky mountain passes of the country. In consideration of my pregnancy, I chose to walk and lead one of the ponies with my daughter in the saddle. It was not the most difficult hike, and I was physically fit and active during my pregnancy. I felt confident that I was not causing any risk to my unborn daughter nestled safely in my womb.

When we reached the crest of the mountain, we had a packed lunch and spent time enjoying the scenery. However, it was not long before our guides indicated that we needed to pack up and get ready to return to where we started our climb. We had not noticed that dark storm clouds were fast descending upon the afternoon sunny skies.

About halfway down the mountain, the rain started, and we all stopped to pull out rain protection or to make other adjustments. We discussed all options to support our small child, protect my pregnancy, and provide a safe descent for us. The trail was becoming increasingly slippery from the rain. We decided that I would ride the pony that I led up and I would support Elena in front of me in the saddle. I took the rain poncho that was provided and placed it over myself and my daughter. As we resumed our descent down the mountain it began to rain harder. Pelting raindrops and darkening skies surrounded us.

I focused on talking to my daughter who sat solemnly in front of me and gazed below us at the steady slow hooves of the pony as he picked his way through the treacherous trail. Then the hail started. Small beads of ice hit my face and bounced off my poncho. It was one of those moments when you think it can't get any worse and you are so in the moment, anticipating the next step the horse will take, and then the next....

We finally made it to the bottom. The hail and the rain stopped. The sun slowly broke through the dark clouds. We had made it. On the van returning to the retreat center, I was quiet as the others excitedly discussed the eventful afternoon. I laid my hands on my belly and felt the reassuring movement of my child. She had been quiet during the descent as if she wanted to reassure me that all was well. I smiled as I thought how one day, I would tell her this story and we would marvel at her tenacity, and the strength of the three of us, together, on the mountain.

Nelson Mandela was released from prison after 27 years on February 11, 1990. Amanda was born four days later. It was a time of jubilation and triumph in SA. While many of the segregationist laws were still in the law books, some hospitals had relaxed these restrictions. I was scheduled to give birth in a private hospital instead of a municipal hospital that had less autonomy concerning regulations. I was sitting in our car while my husband was planning to put money in the parking meter outside of a furniture store. We were planning to buy baby furniture to complete the nursery area in our home. Suddenly, I felt a gush of warm liquid and knew that our baby girl was coming two weeks early and not waiting for her due date. I rolled down my window and said to Graham, "don't put any money in the meter: we are going to have a baby!"

I was barely in the hospital for an hour when Amanda made her appearance after a quick labor. I was much more confident this round, giving advice to the student nurse who was nervously tending to me. I instructed her to get a midwife; unlike midwives in America who routinely deliver babies, these are specially trained nurses who work in obstetrics but assist doctors and do not generally deliver babies.

As soon as the midwife got there and checked the progression of labor, she called my doctor. However, within minutes, she knew she was going to deliver this baby and she did so with calmness and efficiency. Small, yet perfectly formed with jet black hair, my baby entered the world. There was no confusion of what patient floor to put me on, no consternation that the father was a person of color and was hanging around. Times were changing.

Amanda Nothemba was born on February 15, 1990. I had purposefully chosen a strong name. Amanda is my middle name, given to me in honor of one of my great aunts who lived to be almost 100 years old. Aunt Amanda lived close by my family during my young childhood. She kept her eye on me from her rocking chair by the window as I roamed around our country homestead. That rocking chair is now in the home of my daughter, Amanda. She was a remarkable woman in her own right, never marrying, but caring for others' children and serving in other ways.

Amanda's middle name came from my experience one Sunday morning. I sat on a crude wooden bench in a primitive dwelling in Khayelitsha, the largest Black Township in Cape Town, that served as a home for the pastor we worked with and as a meeting place for worship. We served with this pastor to support those living in vast poverty surrounding this space. The pastor was an isiXhosa speaking, Black South African. We met for church in his home every Sunday. It was quite a remarkable phenomenon as we were the only multi-racial church that met at a grassroots level in a potentially volatile Black Township.

Amid despair and violence in the country and in this area, the pastor chose to speak about "hope in the midst of trouble and despair." The word "Themba" was repeatedly used by the pastor and as the word was translated as "hope," it resonated with me. I asked one of the women in the church what the female version of the word was and she told me it was "Nothemba." I had planned to give an African name to my child, and so it was Amanda Nothemba. After each Sunday service, we all stood in a circle outside the dwelling, joining hands as we raised our voices in singing the banned song "Nkosi Sikelel' iAfrika (God or Lord bless Africa)."

The song, composed as a hymn, was banned by the Apartheid Regime as it was used to rally the resistance movement and encourage hope in the struggle for liberation. Hence it was seen as a threat. We sang it to resist the oppression that surrounded us and simultaneously calling for help from God…

> God bless Africa
> May her glory be lifted high
> Hear our petitions
> God bless us, Your children.
> God, we ask You to protect our nation
> Intervene and end all conflicts
> Protect us, protect our nation…

Amanda was born in this tumultuous time when the nation teetered on the edge of hope and despair. For me, her name was a prophetic outcome of the world she would be born into.

However, months later when filing for Amanda's South African birth certificate, I still encountered the same question I had faced with Elena. What "population group" do you want Amanda to be in? The Group Areas Act was still officially law and so her assigned group would determine many legal aspects of her life. I again looked at the legal clerk and said with a bit more emboldened attitude and language, "I don't know, you choose. She has me, a white American mother and a Black/mixed race South African father." This time she was a bit more certain, "Oh, then she would be 'coloured' because her father is 'coloured,'" I mumbled something like "whatever" before I signed the document and left.

Yes, times were changing but for the next three to four years there was immense tension as the country took two steps forward and three steps backward in the march to democracy. As Black people and members of the democratic movement put pressure on the Apartheid government to hand over power, there were forces determined to undermine the efforts. Covert actions were carried out to promote "Black on Black" violence in an attempt to show that Black people could not govern themselves. In response, resistance to these covert actions grew in those who longed for and could smell freedom and liberation. The white military became even more hyper-vigilant in their efforts to quell dissension. Military roadblocks were set up as check points to monitor activity in and out of the Black Townships. They especially stopped vehicles of people who traveled to the Townships but did not live there, thinking they were transporting guns, etc.

One Sunday morning we were on our way to church in Khayelitsha and just as we approached the brow of the hill that looked down over the sprawling township, we were stopped by soldiers. Two young white men, barely out of their teens, wielding large guns, demanded we get out of the car. Both of our children were with us. One formerly chatting from the back seat, now quietly solemn and asking her daddy what was happening, and Amanda several months old, feeding at my breast.

Graham got out with our older child and opened the "boot" (trunk of the car) as instructed. The soldier stepped up to my door and instructed me to get out. I rolled down my window and said to him that my infant was feeding, and the weather was too cold for me to get out. He looked boyishly confused as to what to do when confronted by one of his own, a female at that who was not going to cooperate with his instructions. Finally, as the boot of our car proved uninteresting, and we stated that "we were on our way to church" they waved us through. I can only imagine their confusion when we told them we were going to church among people in the Black townships. It defied all their experiences and understanding.

Later as I sat on the crude, backless benches cuddling my baby girl at my breast I smiled down at her, drew her close, and whispered, "you are Mama's little hope." The intimacy of the moment filled me with joy and wonder. Even with the military patrolling this community, there was a force greater than their military power. The power was unleashed within the primitive walls of that place when we sang together, when we prayed together, and our knowing that my baby and all the children there would one day be part of a new story and would lead the way to freedom.

Graham's ministry responsibilities took him to faraway places. Fundraising trips to support the various social programs he initiated took him to Germany, England, and surrounding areas. He also traveled to remote places in SA for mentoring new churches and encouraging leaders.

During one of these trips to Philipstown that was about an eight-hour car ride from Cape Town, Amanda developed a high fever. Having a sick infant is always scary but facing it alone at night is terrifying. She was generally a very healthy baby, so when she spiked a high fever that would not respond to Panado (SA's equivalent to Tylenol) or other fever reducing measures, I grew alarmed. She was only three or four months old at the time and her little body was hot.

I placed a call to the pediatrician but found he was out of town. His office recommended taking her to the Red Cross Hospital, a municipal children's hospital known for excellent care but also for long lines as it was a public teaching hospital and fulfilled the needs for many who did not have access to preventable medical care. After calling one of my sisters-in-law for advice and companionship, she lovingly came by but did not offer any other options.

As the evening wore on and I put my other daughter to bed, I lay down by Amanda. I had done all the recommended measures of tepid baths, medication, and monitoring temperature, but to no avail. I knew I needed to wait until the morning as I could not leave my other child. There were other community members living with us, but I did not feel comfortable entrusting them with Elena while I would be gone for what I knew would be hours or days.

In the meantime, unknown to me someone in the house put out a call to Graham, over six hours away. I lay with Amanda beside me on the pillow. Being a nurse is a blessing and a curse: knowing potential negative outcomes can wreak havoc in my mind. I fitfully dozed with my finger on her pulse, feeling it race but assuring me that her body was fighting whatever was causing the fever.

The next day as there was no change in her condition, I arranged childcare for Elena and took Amanda to the Red Cross Hospital. I waited in line for hours. Chair by chair I advanced up the lengthy hallway. Baby in arms, I put her to my breast when she cried and observed her for dangerous signs her fever was getting higher. She slept. It did not occur to me that I was the lone white face in the crowd. I guess all my kind went to private hospitals.

Finally, it was my turn. I spoke to the young doctor who was assigned to us. All the doctors were white at that time in SA. I saw the surprise on their faces when they heard my American accent. What was this white American doing in South Africa in these tumultuous times in line at a community hospital? I informed them that I was a nurse and had no intention of leaving my baby's side while she was going through whatever testing they needed to do. I had witnessed all the other parents handing their infants over to the doctors who disappeared behind closed doors. Not happening. After consulting together, they agreed to my presence through a chest x-ray, spinal tap, and blood draw. Amanda stayed extremely calm and cooperative. However, at the end of all the testing they could not find a reason for her elevated temperature.

By that time, it was dark, and they wanted me to stay overnight. I was still alone with my baby. Through the night I sat by Amanda's bed, relieved that they had not found anything infectious but keeping watch. I guarded her arm where the IV was placed and breast fed her every two hours to keep her nourished and hydrated. I felt a strange peace and drew from a well of strength deep within. I believe that God was keeping watch with me and had us in her care. In the morning we were discharged as Amanda's fever had significantly decreased.

Althea, one of the community members, came to pick us up. I felt so relieved to see her smiling face. I found out later that folks had spent hours attempting to reach Graham. The part of the country where he was had very sparse telephone resources, especially in the extremely poor community where he was located. He later told me that he had driven eight hours straight, exceeding the speed limit when he finally heard what I was experiencing. I know he struggled with guilt at times like this, and I tried to assure him that all was well, and we were safe.

I often tell Amanda her guardian angel worked overtime. She was an adventurous child with a free spirit. One of my favorite memories is of her coming home from school and getting changed in play clothes and going outside. She would climb up on top of the six-foot concrete structures on the property that once were used to house livestock. She would sing at the top of her lungs, songs she made up about her pets, about life, about whatever was on her mind. She would sing and walk around on top of those structures. It drove my husband crazy as he felt it was dangerous for her to be up there. I said, "it's fine, let her explore and be free."

When she was about three or four, she had an accident at the home of one of Elena's friends. They were playing around the small pool that was in the backyard. Amanda was playing with dolls in the water and lost her balance and fell in. They were all fully dressed as it was cool weather. She went completely under water. When Elena's friend saw what happened, she dove down and pushed Amanda up out of the water. What could have been a catastrophe was averted by the quick action of that little girl and the watchfulness of Amanda's guardian angel.

Several years ago, Amanda shared with me that she had a dream about this incident. She remembered going down in the water and yet having a deep calmness in her soul. She also questioned why they were allowed to play without direct supervision at this age. I cherish the thought of her calmness amid crisis, and I also carry the question of why we sometimes allowed our children experiences that could have resulted in completely different outcomes. It is one of those divine mysteries of grace and mercy.

Amanda was seven years old when we moved to America. She was adamant that she did not want to leave South Africa. She developed a deep sense of justice and compassion and demonstrated that at an early age. In SA, we lived in an area surrounded by deep poverty. Most evenings several individuals, mostly men would come for food. They preferred to sit outside to eat whatever we could provide for them, sometimes not more than bread with peanut butter or cheese.

Many times, she would go outside and sit with them while they ate. They attempted to communicate with her through the language barrier, but mostly they exchanged smiles and shared human presence. When we moved to America and lived for a short while in Lititz, Pennsylvania with one of my sisters, she asked, "Daddy, are there no poor people in America?" She could not understand why there was no one knocking on the door for food.

Amanda also experienced difficult adjustment in the transition to America. She is very fair-skinned and is often assumed white. She has not assimilated into the white identity that both Black and white Americans have tried to force her into. She fiercely holds onto her South African heritage and racial identity. This is her story to tell as she does so well to those who would listen. She ultimately has transitioned into adulthood with a passion for justice and courage to work toward that goal in whatever situation she finds herself. Amanda has challenged schoolteachers, college professors, bosses, and others who have practiced racism, sexism, and other forms of discrimination even at the risk of losing her job. She is an excellent mother to her baby boy, my wonderful grandson. She lives out the meaning of her strong name Amanda (worthy to be loved), Nothemba (hope) for a better world.

*Dorcas and Graham's parents at Graham's family
home in 1990. From left to right,*

*Back row: Elena, Graham, Luke Horst (Dorcas' father), Hendrick Cyster
(Graham's father. Front Row: Elizabeth Cyster (Graham's mother),
Dorcas (pregnant with Amanda), Ruth Horst (Dorcas's mother)*

CHAPTER ELEVEN

Community

The tranquility of a beautiful summer day in the back yard of our home was disrupted by a stampede of men running for their lives with policemen chasing them. Caregivers grabbed the young children having fun in the wading pool and quickly moved them to safety. The chase continued into the main house, the police overturning chairs and drawing their guns in pursuit.

Graham and I were in the nearby office building when we heard the commotion. We quickly ran into the house to confront what was happening and restore safety. The Black African men running onto the property of our home, The Broken Wall Community, was not a new sight, but the police so aggressively chasing them onto our property was a new level of violence.

Our property was located just down the street from a strategic open field where Black men would wait for day employment. With high unemployment rates, these men represented the poorest of the poor, leaving them vulnerable to low wage jobs and other exploitations. Often caring groups from various organizations would serve soup and bread from the back of vehicles to them. Most times the employment demand was lower than the number of men there, and so they were left in this open field, passing time until the evening hours when they returned to overcrowded homes empty handed. Neighbors had begun to complain about their presence there. They complained to the authorities that the men were urinating in public and generally felt unsafe with their presence there, and the police responded with aggression against the jobseekers.

The Broken Wall Community (BWC) consisted of three formal structures along with two rows of concrete animal shelters. Later, we erected office buildings to accommodate the administration needs of the Community and ministries evolving out of our life together. Graham and I lived there along with other families and singles. The multi-racial, multi-cultural group of people living together in Apartheid South Africa demonstrated that crossing the lines of race was indeed possible, a "sign gift" as it were of what the Kingdom of God could look like. As you can imagine, we drew a lot of attention from the surrounding community and beyond. However, the disenfranchised saw us as a place of safety and refuge. The appearance of people of all colors coming and going and sharing space spoke volumes about the spirit of inclusivity and acceptance represented there. Also, the Black men who led the chase onto the property were from the Black Townships. The BWC was active in the Black Townships, developing relationships with local leaders and raising funds for social programs that the Apartheid government neglected to provide. All this engendered the feeling in those men running into our backyard that day that somehow they would be protected.

In the past, we always knew when a raid was happening up the road as some of the men would run onto the BWC property and the police stopped pursuing. If the men were picked up by the police at this location, they were taken to the nearby police station and held behind bars overnight. This prevented them from the possibility of employment the next day and left their families wondering what happened to their loved one.

When Graham confronted the police that day, he demanded the name of their captain. He also told them that they were on private property, and we had given the men permission to be there. He also pointed out the risk they brought to the individuals living there, including young children.

Later that day Graham contacted the police captain and set up a time that we could meet with him to see if there was a way to resolve the situation. When we met with him several days later, he invited us into his office. When Graham began to explain that we were disturbed by the action of the police toward these men, the captain was shocked. He thought we had come to complain about the presence of the Black men on our property and coming into our home. Graham and I informed him that we had given them permission to come onto our property for such a time as this. He appeared confused that we would be coming to the defense of Black African men. He may have wondered why Graham as a coloured person and I as a white woman were not concerned along with the rest of the surrounding community about the safety risks of their presence. The captain was himself a person of color as were some of the policemen, but Apartheid was successful in denigrating the Black African community to a lower level of humanity than all others.

Graham and I said we understood why the men were on the corner, desperate for employment and wages. We suggested some options such as providing a portable toilet and broader notification to businesses where they could find day labor.

In the end, the captain was cordial and thanked us for coming in. He promised to instruct the police never to come onto our property and apologized for their actions. Sometime later, we noted a porta-potty at the corner field. The men were told they could only wait until noon at this space and then they would have to move. I wish I could say that there were no more raids, but that continued to happen. The men continued to escape to our property, but the police gave up the chase and never followed them onto our property again.

Graham and I founded The Broken Wall Community in 1988. The name came from the biblical passage found in Ephesians 2:14-16, the message of Jesus that replaced the old laws that divided humanity with the law of love and justice. We moved onto the ten-acre property with three other families. It was located at the edge of a farming community directly across from a sprawling coloured township called Lotus River.

Lotus River was developed to house coloured folks after they were forcibly moved from areas that became whites-only areas. It consisted of small concrete block houses and some high-rise project type housing. The area was overcrowded with high unemployment and gang activity. It was not unusual to hear gunshots at night from gang related activity. The farming community that surrounded the back and sides of our property consisted of mainly white farmers in large farmhouses and shabby housing or shacks for farm laborers who were all non-white.

The conditions for farm workers were appalling. Many of them were partially paid with allotments of alcohol with their meager pay. This kept them dependent and docile to all the farmers' demands. There were no daycare facilities, and the women were expected to return to field work weeks after giving birth.

It was out of this situation that I met Mary. She showed up on my doorstep with a gash in her head and a very young baby on her back. She told me her story. Mary was working as a laborer with her husband for a farmer who lived right next to us. One night the farmer wanted her in his bed, but she refused. The next day he put her and her husband off the property with her two children. Mary and her husband were homeless for a few days until they found housing and jobs working in the fields on another farm. She shared how her abusive husband threw a plate of food at her because he did not like the meager meal she was able to scrape together. The plate hit her head, gashing it open. I applied first aid to her head and then gave her some tins of canned food. Thus started a relationship between Mary and me. She would bring me vegetables from her share of the harvest in exchange for whatever canned beans, meat, or other protein I could spare. It is possible the vegetables were stolen: I never asked.

One late afternoon, Mary came to our door with her son Sammy who was several months old. She told me that he had gotten very sick because of exposure to the cold, wet elements of the Cape Town winter. She had to work in the fields even in the rainy season. She could not work all day with him on her back, and there was no one and no place to keep her son while she worked. She had to lay him at the edge of the field on the grass. Mary would put a tarp around him to keep him dry, but he would kick it off and become exposed to the damp and windy weather. In addition, she did not have breast milk, possibly due to her own poor nutrition, and could not afford formula. She showed me Sammy's bottle, which was corn meal with water that had thickened, so he was basically getting water with bits of corn meal residue. She was now very worried as he was lethargic and had difficulty breathing.

I took Sammy's frail body from her and examined him with my stethoscope. Her son's lungs were filled with congestion, and he was struggling for each breath. I told Mary that her son was indeed very sick, and he needed to go to the hospital. Of course, she had no transportation and no money to take public transportation. After discussing the situation with my husband and explaining to my daughters what was going on, I took Mary, the baby, and her seven-year-old daughter to the Red Cross Hospital, the same place where I sat for hours with my infant daughter years earlier. I assisted Mary with checking Sammy into the hospital and taking her place in the long line. I told her I would need to leave her, and they would take good care of her. She agreed.

She asked me if I could take her daughter Rose home with me as she had school in the morning. Mary said Rose was very smart and a good student and she did not want her to miss school. She was so proud that her daughter was going to a proper school and had high hopes for her success and a way out of abject poverty. Mary asked if I could keep Rose overnight, wake her up early so she could go home, change into her school uniform, and then go to school. She further requested that since her daughter needed to go past our house on her way to school, could I pack a lunch for her, and Rose would pick it up as she passed our house. Mary figured she would be home by the time her daughter finished school. I agreed to her plan.

That evening, I offered Rose a bath in our bathtub. She excitedly agreed. I could hardly get her out of the tub when she was finished, and I wondered when last she had sat in a tub of warm water. I made up a bed for her, and she slept soundly. Waking her up early and sending her off to her house, I sadly thought of how this child had to grow up way too soon. I packed her lunch and waited for her to come down the path past our house. Rose smiled when she saw me with her packed lunch. She had put on her school uniform and fixed her hair. She so enthusiastically faced the day. Mary returned home without her son. They had admitted him to the hospital and informed her that if she had not brought him in last evening he would have died.

Several months later Mary asked me if Graham and I would adopt Sammy. She explained that Children's Services had gotten involved in her situation and did not feel that she could adequately parent him given her circumstances. I knew we could not do this. We had our own family responsibilities and at that time were planning to possibly move to America in the years ahead. What would that mean for her relationship with her son?

Soon after that, I lost touch with Mary. As she stopped coming for food, I would like to believe that her situation had changed for the better. Mary was a symbol of women in poverty all over the globe who daily sacrifice their own needs for the sake of their children who they love the best way they know how.

Others came to our door regularly for food. Late afternoon, the dogs would start to bark, and we would see the arrival of individuals looking for food. They came one or two at a time. If we had extra food for the evening meal, we would serve them what we were planning for supper. If not, we would make sandwiches for them. In the summer we gave them water if they needed it, and in the winter, mugs of coffee or tea. In the beginning we invited them in to have their food, but they preferred to sit on the porch or at the outside picnic table. Sometimes we had limited food to meet our own needs, but we always went through the cupboards to offer something substantial, believing that our own needs would be met as we gave of our own resources. We never went to bed hungry like many of those around us.

Crime was rampant in the communities surrounding BWC. Some was based on desperate need. We found out the hard way that anything not nailed down or locked up could disappear. We rescued a worn-out cart pony from the local Animal Protection organization for the children to ride. I proudly bought him a new bright red halter, only to find that when he was at the far end of the pasture someone had stolen it. He came into the stable that evening without it and the reality of just how desperate those around us were was brought home to me in a new way.

We also had several sheep that we brought into a fenced enclosure overnight. One night we woke up to the dogs barking and saw them take chase after retreating figures. The next morning, we noted that whoever the dogs chased off had been busy cutting the wire of the fence to get to the sheep. Thereafter, we kept the sheep padlocked in the small concrete animal pens overnight.

And then there were the fancy little Bantam chickens that one of our daughter's friends had given us since we lived on a farm. The children had great fun with them. One morning a neighbor from the community across the road from our house brought them to our door in a burlap bag. He said he had rescued them from someone who had stolen them and when he saw them, he knew they were ours. He was a friend of BWC and wanted to return them. It was a bit humorous as the chickens were sometimes more of a nuisance than a blessing, but we were touched by the man's thoughtfulness.

The late 80s into early 1990 was an intense time politically. The African National Congress (ANC) was still a government in exile and those who were involved in the democratic movement were still at risk of being arrested. One friend of the BWC who was very active in the ANC asked if an ANC member who was on the run from the police and needed a safe space to "disappear" for a couple of days could stay at BWC. Graham consulted with all the members of the community to see if we all agreed with this. It was unanimous that he could stay with us. There were no details of his name, rank, or duties given as to protect all of us in case we would be questioned. The young man only stayed for a night or two and slept the whole time in a room with the shades drawn. And then as quickly as he came, he was gone. We had provided a safe place for much needed rest and food and were happy to be a stop for one who carried on the fight for freedom for all of us.

The Broken Wall Community was a place of safety to many and to others it was a bone of contention. It represented the possibility that individuals of various races could live together, sharing meals and finances while maintaining their unique cultures. For those who maintained that the "mixing of races" was unnatural and even ungodly, it called for criticism and close monitoring. It was early 1988. The Group Areas Act was still in place that restricted various races living together. We were living illegally. Every aspect of social, educational, and professional life, as well as most religious establishments, was heavily segregated.

We were on the radar of the Security Police, both for our "radical" lifestyle and for the role that Graham played in the resistance movement. Graham had previously met with the Minister of Homeland Affairs to advocate for the entrance of workers and volunteers from other countries to come into South Africa to do peace and justice work. These workers came from Mennonite Central Committee and other organizations that, prior to his advocacy, were banned from entering South Africa. He was asked to commit that these organizations were not going to support violence or engage in other subversive activity. One day two plainclothes security officers showed up at BWC. They asked to speak to Graham, so he took them into his office. They noted the ANC Freedom Charter, as well as the U.S. Declaration of Independence mounted on the wall and questioned how the two were related. They questioned him about non-violent resistance and his commitment to justice.

Sometimes we noted cars parked a short distance from where we lived, occupied by dark shapes, just sitting there for a while and then driving off. At one point the offices of BWC got vandalized. The computers were stolen and files ransacked. We called the police to investigate but no resolution was ever found. Was this an attempt to do a deeper dive into what we were really about? We will never know but we do know that the Security Police often used covert means to find information that they could then use against their targets.

One such covert action really hit home. Some members of the BWC were involved with an organization called the National Initiative for Reconciliation (NIR). It was largely a Christian organization committed to dialoging about injustices between Black and white and finding meaningful ways to rectify these injustices. One weekend we went away for a retreat together. After one of our more meaningful sessions, one of the young women requested an opportunity to wash the feet of those attending. Foot washing is an act used by some religious groups to symbolize humility to brothers and sisters in the faith as demonstrated by Jesus when he washed his disciples' feet. She emotionally expressed to each one after washing their feet why this was important to her and what that person meant to her. She was a white Afrikaner. As one of the privileged, dominant, white minority culture, this act seemed to be a humble act of contrition. She continued to be part of this organization. A couple of years later, we found out that she was actually an informant for the Security Police. I could never understand how she could use a moment so sacred to gain trust and hence secure information to pass onto the government.

The BWC was even repudiated by religious organizations. One publication by an organization called The Gospel Defense League named The Broken Wall Community as a ministry promoting socialist/Marxist ideals. It condemned the practice of sharing resources and finances as too radical and not biblical.

What is a blessing and encouragement to some can be a curse or threatening thing to others. That is what the BWC represented. More than the external manifestation that Apartheid was a myth, the deeper threat was that it was changing individuals' lives. Those that lived there or were touched by the services of the community were breaking down those barriers in their lives. They in turn were affecting others and so the bedrock of separation was being disproved. It was not a simple process and demanded sacrifice as long-standing prejudices and fears were being confronted and healed.

The Broken Wall Community

CHAPTER TWELVE

Life Together

"Community" is a word that represents a feeling. It represents a way of being with one another. Two influences on my life-calling to community have been the writings of Dr. Scott Peck[4] and the concept of Ubuntu. Dr. Peck defines community as "a group of individuals who have learned how to communicate honestly with each other, whose relationships go deeper than their masks of composure, and who have developed some significant commitment to rejoice together, mourn together…and make other's conditions our own." Ubuntu is an African word sometimes translated "I am because we are," capturing the essence of each person being an essential part of humanity and valued for their own unique gifts.

Graham and I had our own unique community experiences for seven years prior to meeting each other: his was in Great Britain in a predominantly white lifestyle community, mine was a predominantly Black experience in Jackson, Mississippi. When we met, we shared this common ideal especially as it was applied to marginalized communities. Individuals that joined us at The Broken Wall Community attempted to live this life of community together.

Althea was one of the first members to join us. She came into our lives at the age of 16. She was part of the youth group

---

4   The Different Drum by Dr. Scott Peck

that Graham and I led at a local church. She is mixed race and identifies herself as Black. In the 1980s, the public schools were a central part of the struggle for liberation. Student Representative Councils (SRCs) were student bodies that resisted the oppressive regime of the Apartheid government, especially as it pertained to educational issues. School boycotts and other nonviolent forms of defiance were implemented but served to only bring more repressive action by the police. Police often entered the school grounds and interrogated the youth about student leaders and "revolutionary" activities. The students were harassed, chased, and sometimes beaten by police. Some students retaliated with stones and setting fire to tires near school grounds to prevent police vehicles from entering. Althea's involvement with the SRC placed her in the heat of the struggle. Althea's parents did not support her involvement in the SRC or other "political" activity out of concerns for her safety. Many parents faced the struggle of wanting to protect their children from getting arrested or injured by the military police and yet supporting the need for change within the country.

    One day Althea showed up at Graham's and my house with suitcase in hand. She was leaving home. Graham and I subsequently initiated dialogue with her and her parents that ultimately made it possible for her to return home and still be involved in the SRC. Althea later lived with us at the BWC after her graduation from high school and then attended college in America with a scholarship that was arranged by Graham through the Tutu Foundation, a scholarship fund set up by Rev. Desmond Tutu for students to study abroad. She returned years later after graduating and lived at the BWC. Althea supported me in those years by loving and assisting with our children. I will forever remember the morning after the long dark night at Red Cross Children's Hospital with my infant daughter

Amanda. Seeing Althea's smiling face when she came to pick us up brought tears of relief and joy to my eyes.

Althea met her life partner at BWC, a young man from Germany who came to visit out of interest in the work BWC was doing in South Africa. Today she recounts the rage that made her stoop to pick up a stone in retaliation to police brutality and has integrated the importance of rage in contributing to the process of transformative healing and voice for justice. While she grew up being taught and believing that anger is a negative emotion, her "freshest thinking" is that anger is a valuable emotion that motivates change and healing. Her life work is dedicated to assisting others on this journey.

Althea wrote the poem below for me as our relationship grew. I was her first encounter with a white person in a shared relationship, one who was willing to share the pain and heartache of a young Black woman facing the many challenges of Apartheid South Africa. Her previous experiences with white people were missionaries and teachers that represented positions of power.

>Dedicated to Dorcas
>
>You came from your white western culture.
>Into my black African land.
>You from your country with its customs
>Into our black land of conflict and stores of
>eruptive hate, governed by black hearts
>camouflaged by white sheets.
>
>So strange instead you became part of us and
>felt the pain, our oppressors oozed within us,
>You touched our blackness and healed our bruises

with those white hands covered in love.

Such compassion and love in a woman like you. You became a friend to me
Through your eyes I saw your heart weeping for the injustices of our land
And in your tears hope is what you brought me,
It was because of you and the love you shared with God above that gave me the chance
to give life another try.
And so, I could once more pick up the shattered pieces and allow them to become complete again.
Now I can start each morning with renewed feelings of hope. Though facing the darkness within.

You helped me trust again
And in our friendship, I learnt how to cope with the feelings
that kept choking at the life in me.

And though I cannot make all those rich promises for our friendship and future,
I will always remember you as the angel God sent to bring restoration to my
broken soul.
"I love you" are words that don't come easily dear sister but that's all I have to give.

God bless.

Nomsa and Siyabulela (Siya) were part of BWC. Nomsa was a single Black African woman, determined but struggling to make it through Bible college and fulfill her dream to be a fully credentialed religious leader. Graham and I supported her and provided a safe place for her to grow thorough the challenges of sexism, racism, and family dynamics. We attended her and Siya's wedding in the rural area of Transkei. This was one of the original "homelands" that the Apartheid government had set aside for Black people with the goal of polarizing them from becoming politically active. Life there was primitive without indoor plumbing or electricity. Vastly different than urbanized Cape Town, the terrain was flat, dry, and barren. Cattle grazed widely and by instinct returned to their own kraal (Afrikaans word meaning an enclosure for livestock) each evening. It was truly a different world and one of the paradoxes within the country of South Africa. A fattened ox was slaughtered for the wedding feast. We witnessed it being hauled from the field in a small pick-up truck that threatened to unbalance and tip over at each turn. We later enjoyed the roasted meat and joined in with the festivities. Nomsa and Siya were part of my life for years and while there were cultural and relationship challenges that required work and commitment, we built a gradual foundation of trust and respect.

One unforgettable experience that demonstrated to me just how strong that relationship was happened at a political demonstration in the middle of Cape Town. It was April of 1993 and Chris Hani was brutally assassinated by right wing extremists in South Africa. Chris Hani was an extremely popular leader within the ANC (African National Congress). His assassination was believed to be an attempt to derail the progressive plan toward democratic elections and liberation for all South Africans.

Days later a vigil followed by a march was to be held at St. George's Cathedral. This was an important venue for progressive religious leaders and was the starting place for the march which was to end in downtown Cape Town. It seemed that organizers of the march grossly underestimated the number of people that showed up to register their grief and outrage at the loss of this leader. Several of us from BWC attended. Nomsa, Siya, and I stuck together while Graham left to support the organizers of the march. This was the first march of this magnitude I attended, as Graham and I had decided in the past that for the security of our children only one of us should put ourselves at risk of being detained or arrested. It now seemed to be a different era of change in how the Security Forces were handling such defiance. Soon the three of us were part of a sea of marching, moving, emotionally charged mass of humanity.

At one point the large crowd separated to make way for a pulsating sea of young people, moving rapidly in disciplined form, chanting and raising their fists. They were chanting in one of the African languages so I could not understand the words but felt the angry sentiment. Nomsa pulled me one side and with a nervous smile whispered in my ear, "do you know what they are saying?" I shook my head no. She said, "they are saying kill the *boer*." She did not need to say more as I was very familiar with the sentiment of the revolutionary phrase that meant "death to the white farmers." In essence, killing those that have oppressed us for so long, in our own country.

Nomsa pushed me behind her as a human shield to protect me. While I did not feel imminently threatened, I realized that I was totally at the mercy of those who for so long had been held down and abused by the evil Apartheid system. While there were other light skinned faces around me, the overwhelming majority were Black, and my eyes opened to my vulnerability.

Siya soon joined us and informed us that the march had gotten out of control. As was the historical pattern, a few of the marchers had begun threatening physical property so the Security Police were indiscriminately firing tear gas and calling for disbursement of the march. As we managed to separate ourselves from the crowd and find a safe way back to our car, we walked into a cloud of tear gas. Shielding our faces and covering our nose and mouth with whatever we could find in our pockets, we coughed and wiped our teary eyes. After a partial recovery, we saw another of our group from BWC who had gotten into the thick of it. I took my tissue and wiped the tears that were running down from his bloodshot eyes. I felt so blessed to be part of a movement that was destined to win liberation despite opposition. I felt so blessed to be with great people. Siya and Nomsa covered me that day at the risk of their own lives. That was community at its finest.

Luthando was in high school when Graham invited him to come and stay at BWC. He was living in one of the Black townships outside of Cape Town. His father was dead, and his mother lived in the Transkei, so he was living with a member of his extended family. The living conditions were sparse and crowded. A community leader introduced him to Graham and spoke about his commitment to education. Graham went to visit him in his home. Luthando showed Graham where he slept and studied, explaining how he would put a blanket over the kitchen table and sit with a candle to study after the family went to bed in the next room. Graham was impressed at his desire to graduate high school and make a better life for himself. At that time many of his peers were forced by family needs to quit school at age sixteen and get a job to help the family. Luthando also was feeling pressure to do so.

We developed a relationship with Luthando over the next several months as he got to know us through visiting our church and the BWC. He readily accepted the invitation to move into the community and to attend a local high school with improved educational resources. He became a reliable member of the community, working hard to complete his studies and assisting with daily tasks. He even babysat our girls on occasion.

One night Graham and I came home later than we anticipated when Luthando had agreed to watch the girls. Our daughters were both fast asleep when we came home. However, Luthando had remained awake, using cold wash cloths on his face to stay awake so he could fulfill his commitment to literally keep an eye on our children. We all laughed together the next day as we discovered our different expectations for "watching the girls." We agreed that the next time just being accessible would include dozing off until we were home.

Luthando truly took responsibility seriously. This was demonstrated by him sending money home to his widowed mother whenever possible that he had earned from odd jobs and babysitting; he initially refused to take money, but we insisted that he had earned it. Later Graham and I got to meet his mother on another trip to the Transkei. She thanked us profusely for assisting her son and supporting him in his goals to graduate high school and develop a career.

Luthando did graduate with high marks and went on to become a manager at the furniture store where he had worked as a clerk. He lived at the BWC for several years and helped to develop the Student Project. This program assisted motivated students from the Black community who were recommended by community leaders. The goal was to break the cycle of dropping out of high school to find employment to benefit the family with their wages. It was a fine balance between pioneering a new method to break generational poverty and respecting the traditional culture. These young people had to find their way through this. Luthando was a great role model.

Some aspects of our life together were uncomfortable. My values as a white American nurse sometimes conflicted with the values of those I lived with. One example of this is how we handled medical care and the need for compliance with the treatment plan. Pumla and Sam were a Black African couple who lived at the BWC for several years. They had three children. Sam often managed the care of the children as Pumla was a schoolteacher and worked through the week. Sam was a pastor.

They had a toddler boy baby who got very sick with chest congestion. I observed his condition getting worse as the days went by with Sam giving him home remedies and over-the-counter medication to treat it. I carefully shared with them my concern for the situation and how his infection could develop into a serious illness, especially with the wet Cape Town winter conditions. I offered to make an appointment for their son with the pediatrician I used for our children. Sam reluctantly said that they would not be able to afford the cost of the visit. I told him that the doctor we used had a policy of not charging clergy for care; Dr. Singer was a Jewish pediatrician who treated all those who came to him regardless of race, etc. I suggested that Sam let the practice know that he was a minister, and I felt sure that would mean no charge. If not, the BWC would help with the cost. Sam requested that I make the appointment. I made the first available appointment which was in a couple of days. After the appointment the couple reported back to me that the baby was diagnosed with a severe chest infection, bordering on pneumonia. The doctor said that if they had not brought him in when they did, he would have required hospitalization. He was prescribed liquid antibiotics for the next 10 days.

As we interacted the next day or so, Sam informed me that their son hated the medication, and it was difficult to make him take it. I stressed how important it was for him to be given the medication as directed and to complete the whole course. He chuckled and said that it was difficult and that the baby was feeling better. The nurse in me was conflicted with what to do. It was obvious that the medication was not being given as prescribed when he showed me the bottle that was more than half full. Should I respect them as parents and just go with the flow? What about the risk to the kid? I knew the illness could persist and most likely get worse due to the irregular administering of the antibiotic. Here I was, the white woman, trying to tell them how to take care of their son.

I decided to have an open talk with them about the situation. I sat down with both parents and gently explained my position and the risks to their baby. They both smiled and stated that he just would not take the medicine and they didn't want to force him. I asked them if they would allow me to give it to him. Without hesitation, they agreed. I took him in my arms and firmly held him and administered the medication despite his protests. Of course, some of it got everywhere, but I was used to that, both professionally and with my own children. It was what needed to be done!

It felt awkward and invasive as I entered their home for the next several days to perform the task of giving their son his medication until it was completed. Sam and Pumla would smile, almost bemused at this woman who was such a stickler for the medication regime. The only thing that kept me going was my concern for their son and that the chest infection would be completely resolved. It was and they were thankful. Our relationship survived this test.

Both families were blessed by our life together. Their children learned English at an early age which served them well in the New South Africa and propelled them into great careers. They learned confidence in rubbing shoulders with children of other races. Sam and Pumla were able to buy a house and get established comfortably. Our children had playmates and developed a natural openness to those of a darker shade of skin than theirs. I learned so much from our life together in sharing economically, respecting differences, and willingness to learn from those differences.

Malvern was a young student with a challenging past who became part of BWC. He was highly intelligent and motivated to defy the barriers that life afforded him. Fatherless and with a mother disabled by a stroke at an early age leading to a premature death, Malvern was orphaned. He grew up in the squalor of the Cape Flats area known as Lotus River, located directly across the road from BWC. His racial background was mixed race or coloured. A Black African woman took him and his disabled mother in and cared for her until her death. This woman was an incredible woman of faith and opened her small home and heart to those around her who were destitute. Malvern remained living with this woman until he moved into the Community. A gentle, caring young man, he graduated with high marks and completed a community college degree.

He was uniquely able to cross the lines between the Black and coloured communities.

I developed a close relationship with him and mentored him as he grew emotionally and spiritually. BWC became his home, and we became his family. He became an integral part of the Student Project and effectively mentored the students as he understood the many challenges they faced.

Another tragedy and incredible loss entered Malvern's life. His brother was fatally stabbed by another gang member. Malvern never spoke much about his brother to me, and yet it was obvious he cared for him deeply. Gang membership had incredible pull in their community, but Malvern rejected that pull and poured himself into his education. Unfortunately for his brother, the lure of belonging and power drew him into this lifestyle.

Graham and I attended the funeral service. It was sad to witness the life of one so young die so senseless. At one point after the service Malvern disappeared. I went to find him. There he was sitting outside, a short distance from the crowd. He was crouched on the curb by the side of the road with his head in his hands. I went and sat down beside him and put my hand on his shoulder. He caved into my arms and wept. As tears ran down my face, I wondered how much grief one person could take before they broke.

Malvern did not break. He went on to touch the lives of many individuals through his work with online humanitarian efforts throughout the continent of Africa. He identifies himself on his Facebook page as a "Goodwill Ambassador." Years later I received word of his untimely death in his 30s. The only contact I had maintained since leaving South Africa with Malvern was an occasional phone call and exchange on

Facebook. I attempted to connect with him when we visited South Africa but was unsuccessful. I wonder now if it was his way of shielding me from the decline in his health. It seems that his kidneys failed him, and he was on dialysis for years prior to his death. I also learned that Malvern often felt lonely, and I now believe that I may have minimized how significant to his sense of belonging BWC, Graham, and I were to him. I still mourn the loss of this soft-spoken, deeply caring friend. I believe he is at peace.

An integral part of BWC was the presence of volunteers from overseas. They came from Great Britain, Germany, and the U.S. Some stayed for years, others for shorter times. I learned a new dynamic of hosting well-intentioned volunteers, as Graham and I were responsible for seeing to their comfort, education, and conflict mediation related to their life in South Africa. Some came with ethnocentric ideas that clashed with African culture and values. Some came ready to serve and learn from the communities they served. Some came with wealth and the backing of wealthy Western organizations and the desire to maintain control with that power. Still other well meaning "missionaries" came with empirical knowledge of what ministry should look like. Through all these experiences, Graham and I developed the stipulation that anyone coming to volunteer needed to bring the funds or resources to support whatever project they were doing and to leave something behind for the communities they served: something real, tangible, and useful as stipulated by the local community leaders. Many of these individuals and groups were a blessing. Some challenged local leadership and behaved irresponsibly as youth breaking free far from their own family and cultural restrictions. It was exhausting at the worst of times; it was rewarding at the best of times.

Community with different races/cultures in 1988 in South Africa during the height of Apartheid was a bridge too far for most white South Africans. The original families who began building a relationship with Graham prior to our marriage and return to South Africa gradually pulled back from the vision of life together. They were okay with outings together and talking about community, but the idea of sharing space and exposing their family life to this radical adventure was a hard stop. Through the twelve years of our life there, only one or two white, South African, single, young people shared various aspects of our multi-racial community for a time. Several other white South African, adults served as advisors or mentors to individuals, but there was too much sacrifice to embrace the vision completely.

Regardless of this phenomenon, BWC served as a beacon on the hill, a glimmer of hope to many who never thought it was possible for persons of all races to come together and live. The idea that faces of different color sat around the same dinner table, sang together, played together, and disagreed with one another, and then came together again changed the lives of many. It gave a prophetic vision of what could happen, what eventually must happen, and the courage to continue to fight for it to become a reality. The young people who witnessed that vision through the Student Project, the BWC, or the involvement in the townships where the poorest of the poor lived, went on to carry that light into their careers, their assertive leadership roles, their marriage relationships, and with their children. The spark that was ignited rebuked the myth that they were less than anyone else because of where they had come from. That spark ignited a fire that continues to burn brightly in many of their lives today.

Children at the Broken Wall Community

Life at the Broken Wall Community required everyone working together.

Family fun in the Cyster's backyard

CHAPTER THIRTEEN

For Better or Worse

It was getting late. I was in bed with a book, waiting for my husband to come home. My two-year old daughter and I had been waiting to greet him, but as her daddy's absence went long past her bedtime, I had tucked her into her bed and resumed the wait alone. It was a vigil to keep the light on until his return from a protest that he and others from the Mass Democratic Movement had organized.

Graham had been involved in political protests ever since I met him but the intensity in these protests had increased in the last several years. As the current white, minority government was feeling the international pressure and local resistance within the country to dismantle Apartheid rule and hand over power, they became more aggressive in their tactics to suppress such protests. Graham had left home at 9 am that morning. It was now dark and past 10 pm at night. I had received a call earlier in the afternoon informing me that Graham along with many others had been arrested and were being held in a local police station. There I was, pregnant with our second child, hoping that no harm would come to their father. September 2, 1989 would be a day that history and I would remember.

The Mass Democratic Movement was an ecumenical movement led by Archbishop Desmond Tutu and other religious leaders including Jewish rabbis and Moslem clerics. Graham had been invited by one of Rev. Tutu's assistants to help with crowd control to minimize chaos if things took an unexpected turn. The march was to begin at the downtown cathedral in Cape Town. The peaceful march of defiance against Apartheid would end at the House of Parliament. The South African police were unpredictable in their response to non-violent actions for justice and resistance to Apartheid, especially now as new hope was gaining for liberation. The world was watching so they no longer used live ammunition but were known to resort to whips, tear gas, rubber bullets, and other forms of brutality to disperse demonstrations.

Relief came to me as I heard Graham's tread coming up the steps to our family's living quarters. I quickly got up and opened the door to greet him. He looked haggard but broke into a warm smile as he wrapped me in his arms. I immediately noticed purple marking all over the jacket that he had worn against the cold Cape Town winter. I asked about the purple stains. Later as we lay in each other's arms he recounted the events of the day.

The police had tried to prevent the marchers from reaching the Houses of Parliament. As the police line barricaded further movement, the religious leaders at the front of the march knelt and began to pray. All religions, praying in their own way, peacefully resisting. The police commandant was not impressed and informed the marchers, "this is an illegal gathering, and you have one minute to disperse." The marchers remained steadfast. The police then unleashed their anger by drawing their whips and spraying teargas. Chaos ensued as the marchers frantically ran for cover.

As Graham ran with others who had reached out to him for direction, including two nuns who thought his large frame would protect them, he looked back and saw a police water canon spraying purple dye into the fleeing demonstrators. He attempted to cover the two nuns with his body to keep them from getting sprayed. He successfully prevented the Catholic sisters from getting the discriminating purple markings, however he was clearly marked by the purple liquid. He proceeded to lead those that had followed him to previously agreed on rally points for regrouping and safety. However, when they arrived, they were met by police vehicles who were arresting all those who carried the purple markings. It was a new strategy to identify all those who participated in the demonstration. Graham was ordered into the vehicle that already contained other demonstrators, and they were taken to a downtown police station.

At the police station hundreds of protestors were herded into several jail cells. There was standing room only. The religious leaders tried to keep the crowds calm and prevent panic from settling in. What transpired in those several hours of detention was described by my husband years later as "true church." Christians, Muslims, and other religious persuasions joined in familiar choruses, freedom songs, and hymns. It boosted morale and hope. The guards ordered the singing to stop, but the detainees were unstoppable. Ten hours later all the demonstrators were released after pleading guilty and signing their names to some minor charge constructed by the magistrate. Designated drivers delivered them safely home.

This day would be remembered in history as the "Purple Rain Protest." [5]

I knew soon after I met Graham, and we began to pursue a relationship that life would be anything but ordinary with him. We were opposite in so many ways. I was a participant in church mission work, Graham was a recipient of American missions outreach. I was a conservatively raised white girl, he was a brown child of Apartheid with the energy of resistance in his blood. Our personalities are vastly different: I am rather introverted, desire not to be noticed, quietly going about my business while he is an extrovertish, full of humor, boisterous, notice-me type of guy. I am a homebody while he loves to travel the globe. We defied all the classic litmus tests for compatible partners. And yet, through our brief courtship that included much intense, honest communication, we discovered our hearts were going the same direction in relationship to our divine purpose, values, and goals.

The tension between being affirmed and liked by people and yet a pioneering spirit that challenged many of the things I had been taught as a white person, has always been a fine line for me. For Graham, it was no question. He was born a middle child in 1948, the year the repressive National Party came into power and divided the nation in so many ways. The limitations and oppression of Apartheid gave him no choice but to call out injustice both as a Black man and as a Christian. Unlike most of his nine siblings, he was never afraid to test the limitations that South African society placed on him. His siblings largely fell in line whether from fear, successful subduing missionary Christianity, or just protecting the advantages in being one level better off than Black African South Africans.

---

5   en.m.wikipedia.org/wik/Purplerainprotest

I remember one of his sisters spontaneously expressing to me, "Graham was always the 'black sheep' of the family" before she stopped herself from saying more. She said this without apparent rancor or malice, but rather logical explanation for why he defied many of the family norms.

He was the only one in his family to matriculate which means he passed a final standardized exam after high school. He went on to Bible school in South Africa, then completed undergrad at a U.S. Bible college, completed two master's degrees at Fuller Theological Seminary and Kings College in London, England, and finished a doctorate at Pacific Western University. He defied the apolitical stance of his church and family. This stance within the Baptist Union of South Africa, a product of British colonialization, in which he had been ordained strained his relationship with Baptist peers and several of his family members who were active within the evangelical Union. It ultimately cost him his position of ordained minister within the denomination when he refused to accept compulsory participation with the Baptist Union Pension Plan. His refusal was to protest the unequal payout to retired pastors based on race. He was asked to appear before the Executive Committee who refused to grant Graham's request to record the meeting, and no minutes were taken. He was ultimately voted out of the denomination due to political stance and activity. He was "defrocked."

One of Graham's colleagues years later described him as a "lion and a dove." The lion inside was fueled by his passion and anger at injustice when it was leveled at him and when he saw it happening to others, especially those who were powerless. While it was not in Graham to display his anger as physical violence toward others, it manifested itself in honest and powerful communication as various platforms arose. It inspired social action that was aimed at political and religious systems and produced radical vision for reform. Often throughout Graham's life of ministry, white folks have found the "lion" side of him threatening, cautioning him to slow down his vision, or to use more nuanced language, often saying, "change takes time" …after decades of little or no change. They loved the dove side of him. Black anger or passion most often is seen as a negative, and an excuse for others to abscond from taking it as a starting place of truth from which effective relationship and peace building must begin. I remember how much sense it made to me when I first heard the analogy Graham used to describe this phenomenon. He described the imagine of a Black man standing against a wall with both hands tied behind his back and then someone repeatedly hitting him. The Black man responded in anger, lunging at the offender. The person responsible for the offence said, "Now, don't get angry" and continued to constrain and hit him. The dominant power group in any context is threatened by the power of anger in those who are being oppressed. Their response is to quell any act of defiance or challenge to the existing status quo no matter how unjust or evil. Conversely, the anger that fuels the power of dominance and control is somehow seen as divine or legitimate, even God-given!

Anger is a secondary response to hurt and pain. It is a healthy response to abuse. It is a powerful form of resistance and a catalyst for change when used with discipline and purpose. At one point in Graham's ministry, he had the opportunity to serve as the youth pastor in a large, multi-racial Anglican parish in South Africa. It was in the late 70s when South Africa was in the heat of the struggle against Apartheid.

Students were demonstrating against the oppression and getting shot, beaten, and detained. This turmoil affected many of the youth that Graham was pastoring. Youth of color were experiencing the violence against them, while the white youth were unscathed.

In an attempt to build understanding between their lived realities, Graham tried to provide opportunities for them to engage in open communication and begin to build more honest relationships and hopefully bring solidarity. After several somewhat successful attempts in which meaningful communication happened, his boss requested an urgent meeting. Graham was instructed to stop any type of further multi-racial interactions between the youth. Graham's white boss gave him no recourse to explain his vision and pulled the power card to stifle any further action for peaceful and effective action between the two worlds.

Graham was devastated. For him, this was the last hope he had for contextualizing all his training and passion to make the gospel real in the fire of violence and oppression. His choices were to internalize the smoldering anger that he felt inside or join those who were fighting injustice by violent means. The pain of seeing the youth from his community get brutalized without any means to level the playing field was too much. He knew he needed an out before the trauma would get the best of him. Through caring persons, Graham was referred to a lifestyle Christian community in Great Britain. The opportunity for him in his brokenness to live, work, and eventually minister with this community of radical followers of God changed the trajectory of his life.

Graham's sphere of ministry grew to include interdenominational ministry in South Africa and international ministry in

England, United States, and Germany. His passion and charismatic speaking ability gathered a large interest and following in these countries as the fight against Apartheid in South Africa gained momentum worldwide. Graham lived for more than thirteen years total outside of his homeland between the late 1960s and 80s.

It was while he was living in England that he learned about the Mennonites. He was captivated by the Anabaptist stance on non-violence, peacemaking, and justice for those who are suffering. Graham trusted that that commitment to justice would give covering to the work we wanted to do together in South Africa. He began to build a partnering relationship with the North American Mennonite church.

All this about the time I was pulling away from the Mennonites as my vision of church broadened. I remember warning him after we were married to be cautious as the Mennonite denomination had a way of protecting their inner ranks from those who disrupt the status quo and are not ethnic Mennonites.

We achieved a "partnering" relationship with a North American Mennonite mission agency. We were never accepted as full or even associate members. I would write articles for the Mennonite publications which were dutifully published but there was never the full support or endorsement that Graham had worked so hard to earn. These articles engendered donations to the agency. Some of these donations were routed to Broken Wall Community (BWC) and then to the budding church ministries as designated. However, it was tightly controlled by the agency and consisted of minimal amounts.

I was the designated article and newsletter writer. In one newsletter that was to be circulated by the Mennonite mission agency, I highlighted the situation of Graham being "defrocked" by the Baptist Union. I felt it was important to let our readers know the type of resistance we were up against even from within the church. I was advised by a high-ranking member of the mission agency who was visiting at the time to not include that in the newsletter The mission person insisted that Graham's actions and subsequent "defrockment" could be seen as defiance and not peace-making. I interpreted peace making differently and believed it to include justice and truth speaking if it was to be true peace. To the well-meaning older mission man, I inwardly asked the question: "Peace at whose expense?" As Martin Luther King Jr so aptly said, "True peace is not merely the absence of tension, but it is the presence of justice and brotherhood/sisterhood." I included the "defrockment" in the next newsletter.

We were expected to host visitors who came to "vet" BWC and the associated church and ministries to underserved people. We were encouraged to build relationships with Mennonite personnel stationed in the Southern Africa region. We attended the suggested retreats and team building weekends, but somehow, we never quite made it. Graham would later describe it as "being invited into the house, but not invited to sit around the table." At the time we felt hurt by the hypocrisy and lack of integrity in most relationships with Mennonite personnel but the intensity of our shared struggle with the people of South Africa left little time to indulge in anger: there was too much work to be done. Years later, as we continue to process and express the anger and disappointment at the injustice of our experience, it still deters us from attending Mennonite gatherings where missions are paraded out and applauded.

Sanctioned Mennonite personnel from the mission agency, white North Americans, were stationed and funded to be representatives in South Africa. They were expected to report back on events happening in South Africa. One couple that we were encouraged to build a relationship with, and indeed were promised if we did such networking our church and ministry would be more legitimized, reached out to us. We obediently took them into the community where our work and ministry were. We introduced them to a community of vast poverty and crude shacks, where we met for Sunday morning worship times and utilized the community's primitive toilet facilities. Our family, including our two young children, integrated into the warmth and hospitality despite the language challenges and primitive amenities. After a couple of attempts to acclimate, the missionary couple informed us that they could no longer attend our place of worship. They attempted to maintain a relationship with us by inviting us to meals and conversation at their suburban home. In a short time, we realized that by sharing our experiences of contact with the townships and other political insights, they were gaining the information they needed to report back to the mission agency. And they in turn got to attend a white "liberal" mainline denomination that talked the talk but stayed safely in the white suburbs.

One phone call between me and the wife of the couple finally put me off. I initially thought she was truly checking on our safety as a family and my heart melted. Support and interest were most times hard to come by and so sorely needed. South Africa continued to be in the international news and at the time of this call, things were chaotic. I wonder if that is what prompted the agency that sent them to reach out and check on things. She in turn needed "on the ground" information and did not have that. As I emotionally expressed how precarious our travel to and from the townships was to do our work and ministry, she listened intently. She then openly acknowledged that they were being asked for a report and needed our information. My emotions quickly changed from feeling loved and supported to serving a purpose. I ended the call rather abruptly. While I don't doubt that there was an element of goodwill and human interest in our well-being, my overwhelming feeling was that Graham and I were being used. It felt like a new low, and the charade was over. It only accentuated the reality that we were needed "in the house" but not to partake of the community that sat around the table. We felt angry and hurt that we were good enough to provide a service but not legitimate enough to warrant regular financial support, while she and her husband were being financially supported and protected by their sending agency. It was enough. Graham and I finally distanced ourselves from the relationship.

We were even asked to get a letter from Archbishop Desmond Tutu endorsing the work and ministry of BWC. Graham successfully obtained a letter from the archbishop in which he enthusiastically endorsed the work we were doing. We dutifully sent it on to the mission agency. We never really knew if this had an impact or not.

We ultimately felt we provided the goods: the contact for visitors to connect with the grassroots people, the social services that made those who gave feel good, a safe place for people to stay who came to visit, and a great work for folks to read about and point to as "being involved in South Africa," which was very important at the time. But the agency still held us at arm's length. We surmised that part of the problem, indeed maybe the whole problem, was that Graham was not a "missionary." He was a brown-skinned Cape Town boy, now a grown up progressive, radical minister. He participated in the struggle for liberation up close and personal. He challenged the political and religious structures with prophetic words of justice and truth. He was not particularly liked by white South Africans. And he challenged the historical colonized mentality of Western missions. His studies at Fuller School of World Missions where he majored in Black and Liberation Theology encouraged an already budding ability to contextualize Christian theology to meet the needs of the poor and oppressed. For me it was a theology that I was already living and embracing. Together, we were a formidable couple, and they did not know what to do with us.

    I recently finished reading a book entitled *An American Martyr in Persia…the Epic Life and Tragic Death of Howard Baskerville.* [6] This true story recounts the transformation of a young Presbyterian missionary to Persia (now Iran) in the early 1900s. As his eyes and heart are opened to the true plight of the people he is called to serve, his mission changes. Through his relationship with the Persian people, he questions his prescribed mission to "spread the gospel" and joins the grassroots struggle to revolt against the corrupt, brutal, and exploitative dictatorship. The North American Mission Agency that sent him disowned him and labeled him a heretic. His transformation ultimately cost him his life.

    As I read this book, I had new clarity about why Graham and I were handled as we were in South Africa. Mennonite missions, as many others, do not want their missionaries to get into messy conflict. The missionaries are to stick to their

---

6   An American Martyr in Persia by Reza Aslan

assignments and operate under the radar as it were. Also, those who win the glory are the ones who stay clean and out of the fray. While this book highlighted a situation well over a century ago, there are vestiges of this history that still haunt North American mission efforts.

While I believe that there has been *some* progression of American mission, I read the book and was struck by an incredible relevancy to our situation in South Africa. In my experience, missionaries are not to get involved in conflictual situations with the local struggle. They are not to take sides. The North American Mennonite man that we were supposed to build a relationship with has become a "peace-making guru" in some church circles. While in South Africa, his training mandated him to teach a "win, win" approach to justice and peace-making, one where each party feels they have equally benefited from the arrangement. He knew better than to bring this to the Black townships where the freedom fighters were actively trying to overthrow the unjust government. How can there be a "win, win" situation when oppressed persons of color were getting killed and beaten by a heavily armed and powerful minority government? For the first time as a white American, I was learning that one must defy the powers that be if their laws are unjust and discriminating. Graham as a SA citizen, howbeit, without a vote, had no option but to apply a contextual reality to faith and justice. Resist. To remain neutral was siding with the oppressors. Missionaries had many other safe options, and when things got too violent, they could retreat to the safety of white enclaves.

Graham never got the trust and full endorsement from the Mennonite church that he desired, hoping it could expand the reach of BWC. However, the money that he raised in fund-raising trips to Germany, England, and other parts of Europe as well as individual donors from the United States, touched many lives. Over twelve years, Graham generated hundreds of thousands of dollars that benefitted numerous daycares and preschools, high school students, and many other social needs of impoverished communities.

Graham was first introduced to Mennonites in Great Britain in the late 70s and was attracted to their stance on peace and justice issues and sense of community. While they marched against Apartheid in Great Britain, the police protected and assisted their efforts, so in reality their commitment was never tested. However, he envisioned that aspects of the theology could be applied to the SA context. Conversely, I had emerged from the struggle in the American deep South, shedding much of what I had grown up with in the Mennonite church that colluded with systemic racism and patriarchy. I remember warning Graham about the clan mentality of the Mennonite church and its pattern of excluding those who advocated for change, especially when it came from those who were not ethnic Mennonites. Against this backdrop I watched painfully as he continued to hope that maybe this person would be different, this next person would accept his authority and truth as a citizen of South Africa. As situation after situation disappointed him, I tried not to say "I told you so" but felt the pain with him. Particularly painful and disappointing was when American Black people were co-opted into visits and did not stand with him as a "brother." I watched as he received rejection after rejection and yet never wavered from his vision. Approval is addictive, and I craved that addiction for most of my life: this dance between doing the right thing and realizing that many times doing the right thing is isolating.

My experiences in South Africa and being married to a man with prophetic gifting has severely challenged and ultimately brought wisdom and balance to the dance.

While Graham loved the opportunities to travel and raise funds for the needs of his homeland, he was also aware of who he was leaving behind: his wife and children. Many of those involved in the struggle against Apartheid faced the dilemma of leaving family for the work of the greater good. It was not one that Graham took lightly and one that we as a couple had to evaluate consistently. One particularly long trip of almost five weeks from home brought a lesson that changed his travels. Our oldest daughter learned to walk while he was away. Just under one year of age, she was joyously toddling around the airport while we waited for Graham's flight to arrive. When he arrived, he squatted down and put out his arms for her to come to him. She walked right by him and lifted her arms up for me to pick her up. Hiding her face in my neck, she shyly peeked out at him. It took some time before she recognized where he fit into her life. Dismayed, Graham remembers this time as a time when he decided that his travels needed to be shorter and less frequent.

Graham was/is an excellent father. He enthusiastically engaged in all aspects of parenting and household responsibilities. He was/is perfectly comfortable in the kitchen and is a wonderful cook. On the other hand, I am comfortable doing outside chores and gardening. One community member laughingly noted one afternoon when Graham was preparing an evening community meal in the kitchen and I was outside caring for the sheep that we break the mold for male/female roles. Indeed, we did break many roles and that is what made us work, together.

Many years later Graham would continue to face the ugliness of racism within Mennonite church organizations. This time on another continent, oceans away from South Africa in America. For approximately ten years, he worked with Mennonite para-church organizations. Visiting church plants in the deep South and mentoring those who were leaders, he developed a vision for strengthening and deepening those in leadership, particularly those leaders of color. He listened and understood their unique challenges with white power structures. Invariably when he advocated for change and handed in reports that included feedback that challenged the status quo of missions, brotherhood, and genuine inclusiveness of minority groups, he was sidelined. On more than one occasion, I got involved in leadership discussions on what racial/social justice would look like within religious bodies. We were told that this was "our thing" and was not a priority for total restructuring.

Graham was told he was not a "good fit" for these jobs and was ultimately let go one by one. This was upsetting for not only Graham but for our family, resulting in economic instability and emotional upheavals. While we attempted to shield our children from the harsh realities, I now know that they had a sense of the anxiety and darkness that skirted around the perimeters of our life together.

In between jobs with Mennonite organizations, Graham had a successful job in Philadelphia as a community organizer. While he found the job duties fulfilling, the daily commute over several years took its toll and he resigned. For some time, he did odd jobs, working at the Mennonite Central Committee Thrift store and then at a Mennonite conference headquarters as a janitor. In between cleaning toilets and other odd jobs, he began to get to know the executive conference minister who led the organization. As their conversations evolved, Miriam recognized and affirmed Graham's qualifications and training. She saw the value of his unique perspectives derived from diverse culture and life experiences and was not threatened by them. Miriam offered him a job as a conference minister, and he accepted. At a staff Christmas celebration that we attended, she officially welcomed Graham into his role and acknowledged that he was, "probably doing more work in the short time he worked there than all of them combined." I remember thinking at the time that this was not going to go down well with some. Unfortunately, sometime later Miriam suffered a health crisis and died. Her replacement was appointed. The replacement was a white male, and he ultimately fired Graham.

This was a particularly traumatic firing, happening just before Christmas of 2011. It happened about a year after Graham was recovering from cancer. He had maintained consistency in pastoring the pastors he was assigned to throughout his chemotherapy regime. During times of extreme fatigue and weakness he would have friends drive him to work-related visits when it was unsafe for him to drive. Graham could sense the relationship with his boss was deteriorating. His academic credentials were being questioned and he was asked to supply transcripts to verify his academic achievements and his PhD title. Strangely enough, this corresponded with the mood of the country, as Barack Obama was being asked to produce proof of American citizenship and academic achievements. Graham refused to do this and requested a meeting with higher leaders in the organization so they could "discuss the situation together as brothers." That never happened. Graham was let go and never to this day received a reason for the firing.

Years later the organization sent him a letter of acknowledgement of the pain and unfair treatment, but no explanation or offer of restitution.

About a year after Graham was fired, we attended a funeral service for a friend's mother. As we entered the funeral home, we saw the church leader who had fired Graham with his wife. We happened to catch up with them in the lobby and realized that we were the only two couples in the vicinity. If there would have been others, Graham and I could have blended into the crowd without greeting them. Turning around to see who was behind them, they stuck out their hands to greet us. Stunned, I was not sure how to respond, but then my "nice girl" attitude took over. "It's good to see you," I said with a smile. As they moved on, I admonished myself inwardly: "*what the heck were you thinking?!*" I just said it was good to see the man who had so unjustly fired and lied about my husband to get him out of the organization he led so he could feel less threatened and more comfortable. Graham, on the other hand, just walked on by into the meeting area without acknowledging his presence. I don't even think he noticed my exchange with this person and if he did there would not have been any judgement. I, on the other hand, have judged myself over and over since then as to why I responded the way I did. If I was there in time again, what would I really like to do? Ignore him, tell him how angry I am at his actions, who knows… There are times when I courageously cross the line, and there are other times when I respond quickly and characteristically "nice" as I was taught to do. On the high road, maybe I just choose my battles, on the road of ease and least resistance, I just say nothing or smile.

After 37 years of marriage, Graham and I often look at each other, smile, and shake our heads, asking the question,

"How did we make it together for so long?" One key ingredient was our commitment to being open and honest with each other or, as Graham would say, "keeping short accounts" with each other. As our journey together progressed, we noticed that because we were so different, in addition to bringing friction that required great work, we developed into fuller people. We also were committed to developing individually by pursuing a journey of healing and growth spiritually, emotionally, and psychologically. We did this by seeking out wise guides at various stages in our lives. We learned to love and minister to others from a place of brokenness and humility.

In the intensity of South Africa, Fridays were our day for play. This was important for sustaining sanity in the midst of what felt like insanity around us. Since weekends were often filled with work including responsibilities on Sunday, we held Fridays as sacrosanct for Graham and me. We took the children to Graham's sister Lottie who loved being with them and headed out for a hike on Table Mountain, a movie, or whatever called to us for those several hours. It proved to be a life-saving discipline for our relationship. Sometimes hikes on Table Mountain brought on conversations that included conflict, so we would create temporary space with me falling back on the trail while Graham pressed forward; we resolved many disagreements and refreshed our spirits. Our beautiful, large, black Lab/Rottweiler who accompanied us on the trail seemed consternated when we parted ways. She would run ahead to be with Graham and then turn around and come back to stick with me, unsure of how to bring us back together into her happy world!

There was only one time that a shadow of threatening to leave ever entered my mind. I don't even remember the topic of disagreement. I do remember feeling that I was not able to get

Graham to even begin to discuss whatever was in question. The children were young, possibly one and three years of age. I looked at them and the way through seemed impossible at the time, and I felt very alone. I remember saying to Graham, "If we can't get through this, I will take my babies and go home." Those words stand out so clear to me, and it's amazing that I cannot remember the reason for them. I do know that whatever it was we were able to find our way through it. After having voiced that sobering thought out loud, there was never cause for it again.

The road has been hard but I have no regrets in choosing to travel that road with Graham. Despite his own personal difficulties, he has always encouraged me to be the woman I am meant to be. He loves me with greater abandonment and grace than I will ever be able to love him. We bring out the best and sometimes the worst in each other, but our commitment and communication is strong and that is what has kept us.

Graham in downtown Cape Town helping to monitor a political protest of Apartheid.

CHAPTER FOURTEEN

Leaving Religion Finding God

The small church was packed. It was the last night of weeklong "evangelistic meetings." I had sat through several of the emotionally charged meetings that were held in the hopes that "souls would get saved", and "numbers would be added to the fold." I was not yet in the fold. The year was 1967 and I was eleven years old. Tonight was going to be my night: I felt the stirring in my young soul. The message was about making a choice to get saved to escape the fires of hell. I believed in my young heart that I was a sinner and needed to accept Jesus into my heart. In that way I would go to heaven. That was more than 50 years ago and although I will never denigrate my first religious experience, my spiritual journey and what I now know to be true has drastically changed.

The next several years were ones of teetering between the safety of warm sweet community as I toed the line of Mennonite church membership and all that entailed, and painful isolation as I navigated the secular world of public school and relationships. These years provided a place to build confidence within the framework of religion. However, as I navigated larger society, including a wider religious experience, I began to change.

Throughout my later teens, I began to do my own studies and reflections on Biblical teachings and information. I began to study my father's religious commentaries which I found on the shelves of his office. I wrote reams of notes of my own interpretation of what I was reading. I experienced a deep movement of the Spirit one evening as I lay in bed, writing my notes about the life and death of Jesus. I felt an incredible love coming through to me. I am not sure if it was what I was writing about, or rather that my spirit was in the right place to feel the Spirit within me calling me to love. A love deep and comforting, that this God thing was not just about escaping hell but about drawing me into a life-changing love experience with the one who created me.

It was around this time that I attended another church service in which I felt moved by a greater freedom to tell this Loving God that I would go wherever the Spirit would lead me in life. I had no idea at the time what all this would mean, but I believe it was a sincere commitment. Something inside of me was changing. It was the first small move to break free from the legalistic religion of my past.

It was also the first time I encountered opposition to explore a greater freedom. This opposition did not come from my parents. By this time, my parents had a larger role in the church and no longer regularly attended the church I was raised in and still attended. I was part of the youth group of the church, and we planned to go away for a weekend retreat with limited oversight from more conservative older folks. As we prayed, sang, and discussed our lives as young people the spirit of freedom and community hit us in a new way.

Previously there had been growing discord among us as some sided with parental pressure to maintain plain dress and other restrictions while others of us were letting these things go. We acknowledged old prejudices and relationship issues between us, forgiving each other, and developing a new spirit of lightness and acceptance for our differences. We left our time together determined to carry our new freedom into the larger church body. We as young people were going to lead the way!

It was not long before the church leadership squelched our newfound joy and awakening with disapproval and warnings that we were being deceived by the evil of the world. I am sure the older church leadership felt threatened and felt they were losing control. They doused the movement of the Spirit with water and put it out. It was not long before it was as if it never happened. It was my first experience of learning about the fear that would drive debilitating status quo and stifle growth. It was soon after that I left the church of my father at twenty years of age. I never looked back.

Something in my spirit drew me to a different type of church experience. In 1977 I began to attend a small group that met in a renovated row house in Reading, PA. It was affiliated with the same church conference as the one I left, but was largely Black, Hispanic, and poor. My life was changed by this experience. I began to see the power and authenticity of Black worship and the struggle that births it. I was blessed to have a strong Black couple as pastors and teachers. I also began to realize the historical racism of the church I grew up in. I discovered that some of the earlier "church plants" were solutions to complaints from white members in white churches that were not pleased when persons of color began to attend their services. Instead of confronting the issue of racism, church leaders found an alternative solution that preserved the peace and reinforced white privilege. I began to see the cracks in church and religion.

In 1979, I went to Mississippi. Everyone was a Christian in the land of the Bible Belt and Southern hospitality. Yet I had never experienced a more openly divided society. For about eighteen months, I was part of the small Mennonite church that was part of my voluntary service assignment. Though it demonstrated the appearance of a multi-racial body, it was not long before I discovered the power and leadership was in the hands of white ethnic Mennonites. As I developed relationships with Black members who were my age, I asked them questions as to why none of them were in leadership. We had many new and interesting discussions, and I believe it empowered them to raise the same questions and motivate change.

In the time I was with that Mennonite church, many questions arose within me as to the purpose of the church amid generational poverty and inequality. It seemed the goal was to put a band aid on the problem and keep people dependent in order to serve the appearance of mission. I had the privilege to work with teenage girls on a weekly basis. While my assignment was to do Bible classes, I realized that most of them already had an idea of what was in the Bible. I centered our discussions around what they were facing in the community, school, and in their homes. We discussed what obstacles prevented them from reaching their goals, and in some cases worked together to formulate goals for their lives. They in turn taught me that pat spiritual answers were not appreciated. I began to see how church had failed them and was not relevant to their everyday challenges and reality.

I did not fit in the little Mennonite church anymore. As I neared the end of my eighteen-month commitment, I knew it was time to move on. My model of developing equal relationships with those who lived in the community was not compatible with the church mission. I observed the mentality in most of the white ethnic Mennonite members as paternalistic and condescending toward individuals from the community.

My ability to build relationships and just hang out with people was misunderstood and sometimes denigrated. One rumor got back to me. Soon after I left, condoms were found in the back yard of the voluntary service house and chapel. Someone commented that it must have been the "Horst girls," referring to my sister and me. We laughed about it when we heard it. I suppose because I dated a Black man and we had open relationships with Black people from the community, it quickly was assumed that we were also having free sex. I remember thinking, if they only knew… *I never had sex in the back yard, but I did make out on their chapel floor!*

Voice of Calvary Fellowship was an inter-denominational, multi-racial fellowship, located in West Jackson. West Jackson was a Black community. Voice of Calvary Ministries was started by Dr. John Perkins, social activist and pioneer for racial justice in the deep South. He experienced arrest, torture, and his family was persecuted for joining the struggle for human rights during the time of Martin Luther King and the Civil Rights movement of the 60s.

While this church was by no means perfect, it changed my life and broadened my outlook on who the church is to be. We struggled with empowering young Black leaders, electing women to key positions in the church, and white fragility when the going got tough. But Sunday morning worship was alive, prophetic in addressing social issues of the day, and reflected Black culture. I joined the gospel choir that was the high point of Sunday services. Rehearsals were once weekly and taught me so much. The choir director was a gifted leader and knew how to pull the deep vocals out of this little white girl. I learned how to rock and clap in rhythm to the songs. We even toured together. Our turned-up volume and amazing harmony immediately enthralled our predominantly white audiences as we travelled through North Carolina. I thought our voices sounded like a little bit of heaven.

My eyes were opened to those from various religious backgrounds, and I learned to appreciate the differences that could either divide or unite. I learned to enjoy a glass of wine and "Pink Champale" (the poor man's champagne). There was an emphasis on community together and less about dogma. Social involvement was a large part of our church life. I went on my first demonstration in downtown Jackson against South African Apartheid. Social programs that assisted housing, childcare, and skills development were part of the ministry life. This was something that felt right and relevant.

The journey of my spirit is never static, and another chapter was about to take me further. My brother-in-law Spencer Perkins, who married my sister, Nancy in 1983, was a leader in the community and in the church but attended church irregularly. This was causing concern in one of the church leaders. One day I asked Spencer, "Why do you not attend church every Sunday?" His response was, "We (Christians) already know what we are supposed to do and be in the world, and don't do it. Why do we just keep listening to more and more if we are not doing what we already know to do?" I wanted to disagree with him, because I was raised to believe that going to church on Sunday was sacrosanct. But the more I thought about his words, I began to agree. Soon after this, Spencer started a "household" group. There were various small groups that met outside of regular services to meet individuals' interests or needs. His was to explore what being in community or living church would mean. This group changed my life. It resonated with what I was beginning to believe was possible if individuals came together in meaningful relationships that were vulnerable and just.

Part of my spiritual journey is one of economic justice. It was in the household group that the seed for economic sharing was nourished. Living in an impoverished community had already started an individual change in me to handle my finances differently. I learned from experience when you are surrounded by poverty and someone "borrows" money from you, you may not get it back. Not because people are careless, but just because there is poverty. I learned that if someone asks for money I give out of my relationship and trust with them that they have a need. If I have, I give. I do not expect it back. If I don't have anything, I explain I do not have anything to give, and the relationship continues. It gets messy if I loan and then it is not able to be paid back. It has been so freeing to live this way.

In the household group we had a practice that after you gave what you felt you needed to the church you were encouraged to give 5% of your take home pay to the household kitty. This kitty was kept for the purpose of anyone in the group who had a need. It could be an electric bill, food, etc. Individuals would be assisted in this way by others who loved and knew them. At the time I was working part-time, going to RN nursing School, and living by myself. Sometimes my

5% was in the single digits, but I gave it anyway. The understanding of rugged individualism, and spiritual bias against the poor as "not wanting to work" had radically changed for me. I saw gospel economy as one of sharing, so no one was in need.

In South Africa, the poverty was pervasive with contrasts paralleled by a racial caste system. It was intended this way to maintain power and control by the Apartheid government. One could not escape it. You were either part of the privileged or part of the oppressed. My journey with economic justice went deeper. Daily I was confronted with the decision to divest what I had and give to those in need or hold on to the excess I possessed. If I had two or three coats hanging in my closet and encountered someone shivering in a light wrap, what was I to do? I literally was tested in the gospel teaching of "if you have one 'tunic' and someone has none, give them one of yours." This was no longer a nice-sounding verse to be read within the walls of a comfortable church, but a front and center test of where I put my faith. I remember handing over more than one coat to someone who did not have one. This concept went further to include my unused tea-set that was stored away after I witnessed a woman putting out chipped mugs to serve tea to guests. I began to sit lightly on "things." Life became simpler.

And then there was the question of safety and how it applies to faith. How much are we required to risk serving the poor or marginalized? In Jackson, I experienced social isolation from some, nasty looks from others, and rumors that I was a lesbian because of relationships that crossed racial lines. In South Africa it was a whole lot more costly.

Every week I would leave my family and drive to the Black township of Khayelitsha. Khayelitsha was a hotbed of political resistance to the Apartheid government in the late 1980s and early 90s, prior to the release of Nelson Mandela from prison. It was also the sprawling shack community where a local pastor had asked Graham and me to assist him in church and community work. I was asked to support the women in their spiritual journeys. We would meet Saturday afternoons. This was a time when the township was a buzz of activity. It was also a time that political gatherings would happen and sometimes community protests.

One Saturday, I had a sense of disquiet as I drove up the slight hill that crested the sprawling sea of shacks. I pulled off the road and turned off the car engine. I breathed a prayer for strength in the midst of fear. I had a deep sense of my vulnerability as a white woman amid legitimate Black anger and frustration. I had been careful to check in with the women to sense the mood of the community and they assured me things were quiet. Yet my anxiety persisted as my thoughts recalled the previous week that had been one of increased turmoil and unrest within the country. Was my fear rational or was I succumbing to the desired effect of the system of Apartheid, fear, and division? I asked for Divine protection as I started the engine and drove over the rise and into the township. Turning off the main road, I entered the dusty dirt road that led to the woman's home where we were meeting. When I entered her home, the women were sitting in a circle on crude backless benches, singing hymns and waiting for me. We greeted each other warmly and the fellowship began.

On another occasion I entered the same area after dark to meet one on one with the pastor's wife who was going through a personal challenge. I still sit with questions about why I was spared any violence or assault. I know others would say that God protected me. But why me and not Amy Biehl[7]? She was a sincere, young, white American student murdered by a rampaging group of Black youth protesting Apartheid oppression. Like me, she was also in a Black township supporting the struggle and surrounded by fellow Black South African students. They tried to intervene but were pushed away and helplessly watched as she was literally hacked to pieces. There is no concrete answer as to why her and not me. I only know my spiritual journey deepened as I began to learn living for the day, the hour, the moment is all we can do, that personal safety is relative, and it is possible to learn to live with it not as a given but as a gift.

Those years were perilous. Yet as I raised my children, going through metal detectors to check for arms or bombs as we entered grocery stores and cinemas, it became part of our normal life. My personal and my family's safety was so much more secure than many others. In the context that we lived, we were privileged.

Even within the church there were threats to the message we believed. One Sunday evening as Graham spoke at a white suburban church as part of his involvement with the National Institute for Reconciliation (NIR), he was threatened by a man who got up and walked out shaking his fist at him. Graham was challenging the white audience to think about what their sons and daughters who were in the South African Defense Force were being asked to do. He was encouraging them to resist going into the Black townships and participating in

---

7   https://en.m.wikipedia.org, https://www.sahistory.org.za>amy-biehl

violent acts against Black people. We were treading on white "Christian" norms that were pillars in religious life.

The NIR was a Christian inter-denominational effort to facilitate meaningful dialogue across racial lines. While it was well intentioned, it never quite broke free from the evangelical doctrine that no longer served the larger struggle for justice. At one of our meetings, we waited for one of the leaders in the liberation struggle to come and share his vision for a new South Africa. Trevor was a person of color, high up in the banned African National Congress. He grew up in the church, had a faith, and was now living that out in what he felt called to do by actively resisting the sin of Apartheid. He arrived late. When he arrived, he explained how he had to disguise his travel route, change vehicles, and enter through the back door of the venue as he knew he was being followed by the South African Security forces. He also had limited time with us as he felt unsafe staying too long at one place. The South African Defense force would have liked nothing better than to arrest him and prevent his further action to bring about liberation. As we attentively listened to updates about the progress being made in the resistance, I noted that one white man who was often very outspoken was restless. Just as our guest was wrapping up and preparing to leave our meeting, the NIR member asked him, "Are you saved?" I remember looking aghast at this man, wondering why he thought a question like that was even relevant at this time and place! Trevor was literally putting his life on the line for the principles of love and justice. And yet in this man's mind, none of that mattered if he was not "saved." Our guest just looked at him, thanked the group for inviting him, and quietly slipped into the night.

My husband had introduced me to contemplative spirituality soon after we met in 1985. I began to read *New Seeds of Contemplation* by Thomas Merton which changed my way of praying. I began to embrace all of life, humanity, and nature as God, believing the Spirit could use all of it to speak to me. For most of my time in South Africa, I met with a spiritual mentor regularly who listened and encouraged me through life's challenges. It became a safe place for me to grow and heal from past and present pain from family, culture, and religion. All was redemptive.

As I grew and became free, I wanted to know more about Spiritual Direction and how I could develop skills to safely offer others this same liberating love and grace. I enrolled in a Spiritual Guidance Program in 1993. The program was conducted by Shalem Institute for Spiritual Formation in Washington, D.C., USA. Two Directors of the Institute came to Cape Town to host this training. It tested and blessed me.

For six months prior to the actual seminar, we were assigned to small groups that met in South African participants' homes. These were called peer groups where we read assigned articles and then discussed them. The articles were on Spiritual Direction/Praxis as it relates to Cross Cultural Spiritual Direction, Social Consciousness, Silence, Gay/Lesbian Community, Discernment, Feminist Spirituality, and many others. We took turns as facilitators. It was a multiracial group as was the larger group that participated in the seminar.

I was tested as we discussed the article on Social Consciousness. The woman who facilitated was also the hostess where the meeting was held. Monthly, I made the trip from my brown side of town to the white affluent suburbs where she lived, opened the high gate that was always locked "to keep out the vagrants," and let myself into her posh home. As she led us in sharing what we had decided to incorporate into our spiritual practice related to Social Consciousness, she opened with what action she chose to implement into her life. She spoke enthusiastically, "In the past when vagrants came for food, I would just give them dry bread. My action of social consciousness is to now put jam on the bread that I give them." I sat quietly taking deep breaths as I knew that I needed to not say anything I would probably regret. I first wanted to laugh at the absurdity of it. Here was a woman surrounded by vast poverty initiated and propped up by people like her. And a teaspoon of jam is all she could come up with! However, one of the main disciplines of becoming a Spiritual Guide is to accept your client where she is at. Our time together was to model that principle. Over time, though, I believe she found herself increasingly uncomfortable around me as the experiences and insights I shared often challenged institutional church structures, racism, and marginalized groups.

The actual weeklong seminar further developed the depth and breadth of my spiritual journey. I discovered the beauty and value of solitude and contemplation. Contemplation as defined by a slowing down, an intentional way of paying attention to ones' heart and soul, especially in relationships, things that make you uncomfortable: socially, culturally, racially, the "other." Contemplation means taking time to mull it over and discern truth, drawing on your Higher Power to give light and direction that leads to action. This is what I began to learn in a new way.

The plenary sessions became heated at times. This was a pivotal time in South Africa. Tensions were high between white and Black; change was coming but at a frustratingly slow pace for many. There was a demand for a spirituality that included justice and equity and the will of all to make it that way. White people knew that change needed to happen, but as history often bears out, the church is often way behind or not even willing to start. Somehow, we all survived and heard each other's hearts through skilled facilitation that provided safe space.

I further participated in Community Building Groups and workshops that were facilitated by trained leaders in Scott Peck's model of building diverse and inclusive community experiences that respect the input of all. These experiences stretched me. No one is regarded as higher or more right than another in these intentional groups that meet for a whole day. We sat in silence until participants were moved by the spirit to speak. The group moves from pseudo community, to chaos, to emptiness, and finally find each other in community. It was powerful. The groups were comprised of individuals from all walks of life, race, culture, religion, and without religion. It was a miracle to see the environment change from trying to change each other or argue a point or instruct or rescue someone else to just being quiet and allowing to trust the process. There was ultimately the humble acceptance of the common human need for community and harmony.

My core being is rooted in authentic community with others whenever possible. I have seen the effects of greed and power in various contexts, and it is never good. As bell hooks writes in her book, *All About Love:* "Worship of individualism has in part led us to the unhealthy culture of narcissism that is so all pervasive in our society…western travelers journey to the poorest countries and are astounded by the level of communion between people who, though not materially rich, have full hearts…we are rarely healed in isolation…healing is an act of communion."

So where am I today? There are those who would say I have lost my faith. I would say I have not lost my faith, but rather religion. I let go of the rigid, narrow, legalistic parameters of religion that no longer serve me. My Higher Power is still God. But a very different God than I was introduced to as a child. I grew up singing "Jesus Loves the Little Children," yet I responded to an invitation to get saved from Hell. That doesn't even make sense. I don't believe I was born in sin and needed to be saved. I believe that I came into my physical being from a place in the cosmos that was full of love and God. And then life happened, sometimes shit happened, sometimes good stuff happened. I believe that our lives on earth are a constant opportunity and draw to join in love with our Creator for healing and redemption. Sometimes we take detours, and we fall, but the love is always there. I believe that God is both male and female and the Spirit (female, Sophia, essence of wisdom, dance, and fun) understands all things about and in us. I believe we are here to be with all humanity regardless of religion, gender, race, or place in society. We are to be champions for love and justice in the most courageous sense of those words.

I have friends from other religions. I do not feel the need to convert them or convince them that there is only one way. I do not know. I can only trust and respect their journey and open myself up to learn and grow from our relationship. I have been encouraged and challenged by my Black, Muslim friend whose faith sustained him through years of unjust incarceration and long periods of solitary confinement. I have incredible respect for my friend who is atheist and lives her life serving others. I have learned so much from friends in the LGBTQ community and share their griefs as they face hate and isolation from society and yet joy from who they choose to love.

I have left the church building. The small fellowship group that Graham and I led disbanded when Graham retired and then the pandemic happened. I have been in church only a few times in the past three years. I do not know where to find a church where I feel safe and am not bombarded with narrow doctrine, where I could bring my trans-gender friend and know she would not be stared at or someone trying to change her.

But I am not lost. The original faith that survived all the onslaughts of organized religion and built on that golden thread of truth is still there. It sustains me through all the joys and sorrows this life affords. I will hold to that thread until I cross to that place from whence I came.

CHAPTER FIFTEEN

Hope and Change

The long lines of voters stretched for kilometers. It was April 27, 1994, and the people of South Africa were waiting to cast their vote. For the majority, it was the first time they had the opportunity to vote. Nelson Mandela was on the ballot under the heading of African National Congress (ANC), an organization that had been banned for decades. The initial jubilation and euphoria of Mr. Mandela's release four years earlier had given way to intense struggle by those who had been disenfranchised for so long and the ambivalence of the white minority government to relinquish power. After various attempts by the Nationalist Party to sabotage the march to majority rule, this day had finally come.

Graham and I were both voting for the first time. I was 38 years old; Graham was 45. My Mennonite heritage said that faith and politics did not go together and so no one in church or family went to the polls. Graham had been prevented from voting by laws that only allowed whites to vote. It was an emotional day for him. Bittersweet, as he looked back on some of the best years of his life having been lived in an environment that considered him less of a human as others because of the color of his skin. Today, he had the opportunity to cast a vote that would put a man of his color in control of the country of his birth.

Growing up I never considered it important to vote. Being "involved in politics" was not encouraged, although it was a given in my home that the Republican Party was the right party for morality and family values. It was in South Africa that I learned how important the right to vote is and indeed a responsibility to be aware of the factors that determined who was to govern. The choice was so clear: either a vote to enshrine the laws of hate, bigotry, and injustice, or one to usher in a new government that would work to bring about democracy. I was not even a South African citizen, but my Identity Document that had a permanent residence stamp, gave me the right to cast my first presidential vote for Nelson Rolihlahla Mandela!

Black South Africans and others of all races who supported the freedom struggle waited expectantly for the vote count to confirm that Nelson Mandela would be the first democratically elected president of the New South Africa. Others waited in fear. Many white, mixed race, and other individuals who had fears of Black majority rule waited anxiously for the worst to happen. One member of Graham's family shared how he was fearful that if a Black government was elected someone would come knocking on his door and tell him he had to move out of his house. It is hard to make others from outside of South Africa understand how successful the Apartheid government was in building fear between racial groups. Some mixed race or coloured folks believed that Black South Africans would retaliate against them because of the privileges they had received in the caste system that Black people did not. I knew from personal relationships and experience that such fear was unwarranted. In South Africa as with Black folks in America, Black people know what it is to be oppressed and are uniquely qualified to arbitrate a government that works for everyone. If there was to have been a "blood bath" as some feared, it could have happened four years earlier after Mandela was released. He would only have had to say the word. Instead, he said, "I have fought against white domination, and I have fought against Black domination. I have cherished the ideal of a democratic and free society in which all persons live together… with equal opportunities…It is an ideal which I hope to live for…but if needs be, it is an ideal for which I am prepared to die." I am truly privileged to not only have had the opportunity to cast a vote for this great man but to shake his hand and look into his eyes.

Jubilation and hope filled our hearts when Nelson Mandela won the popular vote and was sworn in as the President of South Africa. It felt like the pressure cooker of living under Apartheid finally had the lid blown off. Black people now saw themselves in important positions in government, sitting in South African parliament and bringing in new inclusive laws and abolishing the last dregs of Apartheid laws. The Freedom Charter that had been developed by the ANC while in exile and members that were imprisoned with Nelson Mandela was adopted to enshrine democracy for all time in South Africa.

What did this mean for us at The Broken Wall Community? We rejoiced and lived in the spirit of jubilation that political freedom brought. But the reality of what this meant to the shape and life of the projects and ministry of BWC needed to be considered. The new government promised to allocate more attention and finances to childcare and student development. These were the two areas that received most of our fundraising.

The Student Project that provided a place for high school students to live outside of impoverished areas and hence access better schools would eventually not be needed. With the group areas act completely gone and restricted living areas opening, access to better schools would evolve. School fees were eliminated for most public education, making it affordable for students to complete high school. We decided to maintain the Student Project to see the currently enrolled students through to graduation and then re-evaluate.

The pre-school programs that were heavily funded by BWC required little oversight to daily operations with exceptional local administration now in place. The funds generated allowed them to expand to other community needs and provide jobs for members of the community. We anticipated more government funding now available as the democratic government prioritized marginalized communities and needs of previously neglected children.

It seemed almost overnight that the world briefly celebrated with South Africa in the ushering in of the "New South Africa, Rainbow Nation," and then turned its attention elsewhere. The donations from overseas decreased. It was time for an "indaba" (South African word for a meeting to discuss a serious topic). While the governing board of BWC was attentive, they indicated that the decision largely rested with members of the community. As co-directors of the ministry, Graham and I felt the heartbeat of those we lived and served. One preschool leader we worked with admonished us to think about what we as a family needed. This woman had worked with us for over ten years and had seen the sacrifice and hard work that our family had done. She now served as a leader in one of the Black townships, overseeing a large preschool and hostel for neglected elderly residents. Nobuntu had lived out the gospel with us and now told us to see to our family. There were others who encouraged us in this way.

For several years the BWC had arranged shipping containers of clothing, food, medical supplies, bicycles, and other items that arrived yearly from England. Most of the items were distributed to the women who ran the preschools. Graham and I never took any of the contents for our family. One year our oldest daughter watched all the items being unloaded and sorted. She saw a stuffed horse, with saddle and bridle attached, placed on the pile of toys for distribution. She indicated that she wanted it. Graham gently explained that the toys were for children who did not have toys. One of the preschool teachers witnessed this exchange. She kindly but directly chastised Graham and then went and got the toy horse and placed it in Elena's arms. She addressed both of us, "You two have done so much for so many, why should your children not share in some of this?" It was a word in season.

We had given so much for so long, and it was now time to make our family's needs a pivotal part of the discussion. We decided to take the next two years to refocus our lives and the ministry. Graham and I felt that our original vision of a multi-racial community had been marginalized by the immediacy of social needs and the struggle for justice. Rightly so. But we knew that now more than ever, South Africa would need a model of what life together would look like now that political power was achieved by Black people. People would need to learn to work together to build this "New South

Africa" after decades of suspicion, fear, and hate toward one another. We decided that Graham would look for work independent of the ministry. We would see if there were other individuals, or families or who would be interested in building a shared life together.

As BWC gradually disengaged with the projects, the personal support receded as well. The years of 1995 and 1996 had some desert periods for us as a family. Sometime during that time period, I wrote this to our ministry partners oversees in a document titled, "A Testimony from the Cysters." "The phone rang, and I heard my mother's voice on the other end. We exchanged the usual warm greetings…what was happening with the weather, the children, the rest of the family, and the activities that keep us busy each day. Then came the question that I anticipated with some anxiety, 'Dorcas, how are you doing?' What should I answer? Could I say that my heart was heavy and my spirit tired…that I felt God was far away and turning a deaf ear to Graham and me, that I was afraid that our finances would not cover this month's expenses…that I felt alone and forsaken…?" I went on to say that I knew my mother would have accepted the truth in our situation with loving care and compassion but instead of giving her more to worry about, I said I was fine and that "God was faithful."

And indeed, we made it through. Years later that phone conversation reveals the deep emotion of that time in my life. The finances did come through to pay the annual school fees and purchase school uniforms for the start of a new school year for our two girls, to put bread on our table and keep a roof over our heads. But after several short-term jobs for Graham that ended with the economic transition in the country, we knew we had to make a decisive decision to stay or leave South

Africa. One option for Graham was to accept a political position within the newly formed government. While this was an exciting prospect, it did not feel right to him at the time.

During these two years, people who knew and loved what the BWC represented were reluctant to see it disband, yet not willing to carry on the dream. Economic empowerment was the focus of the day and new opportunities had opened for those who were long disenfranchised. Bit by bit we relinquished our roles and handed leadership of the various ministries to others who would carry them into a new era.

For Christmas of 1995, we spent the holidays with my family in America and returned to South Africa in early 1996. Our daughters had made significant connections with their American cousins and our oldest daughter, Elena, expressed the desire to live in America. I remember that as one of the first sparks of conversation that engendered dialogue about leaving South Africa and resettling in the U.S. Conversely, Amanda our other daughter was adamantly opposed to leaving SA. Over time she reconciled herself with the idea.

I remember one breezy mid-year afternoon in Cape Town. I was taking down wash from the line and as I watched my children playing with some of their animals, a clarity came to me. Whether I merely thought it in my head or declared it out loud, I am not sure, but the certainty came together that if we were going to make a move to America it needed to happen in the next year. I remember expressing to Graham, "If we are going to move it needs to happen before the children get too much older because adjustment with school and friends will get harder." At the time, they were ages nine and six.

The ambivalence within me was profound. In fact, if a steady job had presented for Graham or some other certainty had emerged, I believe we may still be in South Africa. South Africa had gone from being a place where I was planted for a season to being my home. I had integrated into my family by marriage, become friends with my sisters-in-law, and supported my father-in-law through an extended illness and mourned with the family in his death. I looked at America from afar and realized that it was the country in which I was born and lived, but I could be at peace elsewhere. While there were aspects I would miss, I was bigger than its borders. While my visits to my family were nostalgic and good, the gaps between our lifestyles and values seemed sometimes a chasm too wide. South Africa was the birthplace of my daughters and no matter how fraught with challenges, it was the place of sea and land, wild and spontaneous. How would I ever fit back into America? How would my family navigate the tendency of ethnocentrism and arrogance that often is part of the American Dream?

However, there was part of me that felt like a warrior returning from a long battle. That my reserves were almost depleted from being dependent on those who gave with sometimes unrealistic expectations. There was a side of me that longed for the familiar. I wanted to return to my nursing profession and feel more in control of my destiny as a woman, wife, and mother.

My daughters had thrived in their South African school experience. They wore school uniforms and had excellent teachers. Their classmates and friends were diverse in race, culture, and religion. Their best friends were Muslim children, whose parents trusted us as Christian parents to support their religious dietary restrictions when they had sleepovers. From their birth they gazed into faces of all colors and were held by arms that were shades of black, brown and white. They had lovely South African accents and swam naked in the ocean as children. How would they ever fit in?

When we sifted through all the ambivalence of feelings and discussed pros and cons of the practical aspects of moving, we finally decided that it was time. We would leave the summer of 1997 to allow time to settle in for the beginning of the autumn school year. That would mean the children would leave in the middle of the South African school year as it ran from January to December.

The last year in South Africa was one of cautious optimism and excitement interspersed with sadness as the tasks of leaving sometimes became overwhelming. We had to find homes for our pets. That was gut-wrenching as we handed them over to those who promised to look after them but could never give them the love we had. This was particularly hard for my daughters and something we still speak about today, until we grow quiet as it just becomes too painful.

There was the unfinished business of working out the prophetic possibility of life together with Black and white now that the laws that prohibited it were gone. This was the original dream that Graham and I believed would truly demonstrate the gospel of love. We knew that the true test was still to come and wondered if there would be those who would dare to take it on. And indeed, today almost 30 years after liberation and a democratic government that reflects the people of South Africa, the vast economic and social gaps remain. Secular business and corporate groups now have mandated quotas to adhere to, but the ability to truly process the generational trauma from Apartheid is dismally lacking. Religious establishments struggle to integrate the emotional and spiritual scars their members carry with them. Brave individuals take on the challenge, but often find themselves on a lonely road with the potential for burnout.

We left with the consolation that we had done the best we could in very turbulent times. The individual lives that we touched and nurtured would carry the torch to touch many others with the hope and promise that true brother and sisterhood was possible if one was ready to do the work. The struggle would continue, with the hope of victories along the way.

I left the borders of South Africa a vastly different person than the 20-something young woman who landed there in the heat of a political revolution almost twelve years earlier. I had matured in my ability to share in my partner's struggle as a Black South African, letting go of much of my culture in order to integrate into the freedom of community and diversity. I had observed and entered the pain of oppression and poverty. I observed the injustice and cruelty toward those who were considered less than human only because of the color of their skin, injustice meted out by seemingly well-intentioned individuals as well as the police. I learned to live simply and acquire what was necessary for life, not how much could be stored up. I had birthed two children in a foreign land, guarding their innocence in a world where many children faced trauma and had to grow up way too fast. I faced the daily challenge of balancing my role as their mother with the vast demands around us as a family. I had participated in the momentous struggle that had changed history for a country and for the world. I was blessed to meet so many courageous and strong women and men, young and old, who refused to give up the fight despite all odds, who stood on the front lines with their fists raised, defying armed vehicles and men. I learned cultural humility, exchanging what I thought I knew for what I will always keep learning.

Packing up our possessions was relatively easy: we lived simply and accumulated minimal stuff by Western standards. Packing up our lives was an emotional roller coaster of saying goodbye to so many and a country that had challenged and nurtured us for over a decade. As the plane lifted off from Cape Town International Airport, I focused on the needs of my daughters. At ages seven and ten, they were filled with excitement and anxiety about what was ahead. Much later, on our twenty-plus hour flight, the cabin lights were dimmed, and things grew quieter. I closed my eyes and connected with my own emotional turmoil. I was going home, but was home still going to embrace the person I had become? Would it even recognize this forty-something woman who had lived what seemed a lifetime in the past twelve years? What parts of me would need to be squeezed and stifled to fit back into a mold that would fit into family and culture…

The racing questions gave way to the peaceful knowledge that I had changed and with that change came strength and resolve. Come what may, I would carry the lessons of life that I had learned from crossing the lines. Those lessons had brought courage that defied restrictive fear and brought me closer to love. And ultimately, love is strength.

Epilogue

Twenty-seven years have gone by since my family and I crossed the Atlantic and resettled in America. Little did we know the challenges that would await us. One certainty that I have experienced is that we only get to see what is directly in front of us as one of the graces of being human. While my family's challenges have been immense, I remain steadfast that for the most part we made the right decision.

My daughters have braved the onslaught of others suggesting what racial identity they fit into. A Black college professor told one of my daughters that she needs to identify as white; others spoke to them in Spanish only to be dismayed at their confused faces. I am continually surprised and disturbed by the ignorance of Americans who look mainly through an American lens of Black and white, with little knowledge of global history. My daughters are immigrants to America, representing a country with its own unique racist system that classified them as "coloured:" they do not fit into an American assumption that just because they may pass as white, they need to comply. They represent some of the millions that leave unjust systems of caste, poverty, and privilege and endeavor to find their place of acceptance within the struggle for justice and human rights. My daughters carry the scars of a racist government that from birth classified them as "less than." They also carry the strength of African ancestors who bred strength and stamina in them. Now as young adults, they are confident and proud of their South African identity of mixed race.

My husband is now retired after years of encountering covert racism in his various positions in primarily religious organizations. Despite that, he has touched the lives of individuals who remind him of how his love and care has offered new hope and direction. His most memorable experience was within the state prison system as a prison chaplain. Several Christians and Muslims who were incarcerated during his time of chaplaincy remain in contact with him. Graham's ability to see them as "brothers" and not just inmates has left an indelible impression on them. A cancer survivor of over ten years, he continues to journey as a wounded healer, leaving the institutional church he loved and believed so strongly could be a "sign gift" of the Kingdom of God, and finding church everywhere he goes.

More than two decades ago, I was plagued by questioning what parts of me would need to be squeezed and stifled to integrate back into my homeland, family, and culture. My relationships with my parents and siblings have been various stages of challenging. Soon after I moved home, my parents moved into a retirement village. My idea of intergenerational living as modeled in South Africa put me at odds with most of my family as my husband and I offered to rework our home to accommodate my parents. It was primarily my dad's decision to move to a retirement facility and establish life with their peers in a cottage on site. Several years later my mother had a stroke, and I assumed a caregiving role with my mother.

Over the next ten plus years, I managed her extensive medical care until she had a second stroke that landed her in the skilled nursing facility. For the last six months of her life, I agonized each time I would leave her: alone but fully aware of life around her, cared for by strangers, her brilliant mind struggling to formulate the words her brain organized. I sat on the floor by her wheelchair talking to her as we gazed out of the large foyer window and observed the changing seasons. I regret not having the ability to have her in my home with appropriate help for those last six months, surrounded by family that she had served so well for almost 70 years. South African culture taught me the value of the elderly in a way that white American culture does not. South Africans believe the elders have wisdom that younger ones are only learning, while the burden of caring for the elderly brings character and wisdom in the doing.

My children also had a different attitude toward their grandparents. Taught by their South African family to always respect and serve them, my youngest daughter spent one day every week over the summer with my mother after her stroke. She still talks about their talks, my mother sometimes struggling to express herself and how that solidified their love for each other even as generational differences arose. My oldest daughter still recounts the difficulty in navigating conversations about "sexual purity" as she approached her wedding day, yet still has a great love for her grandmother. My mother crossed over to the next world in January of 2013 at the age of 90.

I had a similar caregiving relationship with my father as his health declined. He lived to be 97 years old, with the last six months of his life in skilled care. We had a relationship of redemptive conversations and candid honesty in his later years. He openly shared some of the conflicts he had in enforcing some of the unsavory parts of church doctrine, such as prohibiting TV and supporting plain dress for young women in such a radical way. He also expressed regrets about the "salvation" experience being linked to church membership and its demands back then. He expressed sorrow for my experiences as a Mennonite girl in public school. This was quite an acknowledgement coming from a man who had given his life to the church. For me it opened up a freedom and greater love for him.

While there is racial diversity in my family of origin, my family is the only immigrant family. This has presented unique challenges as my husband and children grew up and lived abroad, with a different perspective on America and the American dream. Even American minority groups are sometimes blind to the challenges immigrants face to live in America. My birth family had the predominant mentality of each family for themselves, kind of a "pull yourself up by your own bootstraps" philosophy, antithetical to the African concept of community. The love was there, but just expressed differently and with best intentions.

I could not bring all I had learned into my workplace. I had to constantly discern what and how to be faithful to all that my experiences had taught me and yet temper my passion with where folks were at. I have worked for over 23 years within the healthcare field. I retired in July of 2021 after guiding my team of 23 maternal/newborn health professionals and support staff through most of the Covid pandemic. While I experienced great professors, managers, and peers in my years obtaining higher education and leadership advancement, I also experienced the challenges. I broadened my understanding of health care equity and applied the principles in advocating for and hiring of persons of color to represent the population served. I supported individuals who faced racism or felt otherwise marginalized and isolated within the organization. I challenged the structures as they existed, with the vision of what opportunities were possible if we adapted those structures for advancement of those who were not granted an equal starting place. I won and I lost, but I kept fighting until the end. Institutional racism and bias are real, even in an organization that is so well meaning.

Several years after moving back to America, I felt a restlessness to expand my gift of caring for others in a more holistic way. My choices were to expand my knowledge of spiritual direction that had begun in South Africa, or to enroll in a training program for counseling. Spiritual direction is the praxis of accompanying others on their spiritual journey. It can be done in a group or individually. It draws on the belief that all of one's life is spiritual and can be touchstones for growth and redemption. While I have a healthy respect for secular mental health counseling, it often neglects the spiritual aspect of emotional health. After working with church related women's groups for several years, I sensed the gap between what women were receiving in traditional church and what they were encountering in the day-to-day issues of life. I decided to complete another year developing my practice of spiritual direction.

Once again, I had to cross the line from the traditional, classic approach to this practice, taking it out of traditional places of worship and into the streets. Institutional denominations have largely monopolized the training and practice of spiritual direction, keeping it for those with the luxury to meet at expensive retreat centers or take time out of their daily schedules to meet in out of the way places. I felt alone within the training context as I pondered how to make spiritual direction available to those struggling to make ends meet and survive from one crisis to the next. I was drawn to the concept of group spiritual direction given the importance of collective thought in communities of color.

For the past twenty years, I have integrated elements of spiritual direction practice such as listening and validating each one's personal experience in my role as nurse, mother, wife, family member, and friend. Currently I have adapted the practice to "Spiritual Guide, Spiritual Friend," or other less hierarchical terms, utilizing "Crisis Contemplation" which is a current term that speaks to the needs of many marginalized populations in society. It focuses on leaning into and listening to the immediate need as it is communicated rather than prescribing a set time to sit down in a quiet place. A quiet uninterrupted space is often an unlikely luxury for individuals struggling for survival in difficult circumstances.

Often, I just listen. I may receive a telephone call from a busy mother who needs someone to validate her thoughts and experiences in between transporting her children and attending to other demands on her time. For years I had an opportunity to interact with an individual who was an inmate at a state penitentiary, and our time together was unplanned, depending on when a shared public phone was available. Sometimes a friend who is alone and scared calls me from a hospital emergency room. All of us as humans need a calm voice when we encounter a stressful or terrible situation. It is part of my calling to be there for others, assuring them they are not alone, and joining with them in reaching for a Higher Power.

Our family has returned to South Africa twice since we left in 1997. They have been bittersweet visits. It is a joy to connect with family and friends, but always so hard to say goodbye, not knowing if or when we will again hug and meet in the flesh. At our last visit in 2014, an unexpected funeral service for one of Graham's sisters overshadowed the visit in which my son-in-law was introduced to my daughter's South African family. In the last five years, Graham's brother Clive died abruptly from a massive heart attack and a sister-in-law died from complications from Covid. Clive was like a second father to my daughters and was Graham's closest brother. We are still processing his death as he was the one who arranged our visits and was our main host while we were there. We attended his memorial service via the internet, gathered around our dinner table at 3am USA time to accommodate the time change. We grieved with our family so far away. Clive will always be remembered for his big heart, sense of humor, and acceptance of others.

Maintaining genuine relationships with others from a distance is difficult even in this age of social media and internet communication. I am in touch with a host of South African family and friends on Facebook and WhatsApp and stay updated with life changes. I also maintain close contact with my friend Althea Banda-Hansmann (Broken Wall Community member as described in Chapter 12) since our shared time in South Africa beginning in 1986. Graham and I have regular Zoom calls with Althea and her husband Jurgen; what began as them reaching out to us for support as an inter-racial couple has become an important component of mutual sharing of our spiritual/emotional/physical journeys. Althea and Jurgen are bravely venturing on a road less traveled, integrating social and racial history/trauma with emotional and spiritual transformation. Althea particularly faces challenges as she confronts misogynistic and racist resistance to her wisdom and skills as a Black woman. I have individual Zoom calls with Althea monthly. Together we affirm and empower each other's journeys. Our long history together and mutual respect for the Divine in each other provides a place of deep refreshment and rest.

Althea and I recently experienced a challenge that tested the depth of our relationship. I sent Althea the portion from chapter 12 of this memoir where she was introduced as part of my story. One aspect of my original version mentioned my interpretation of her rage in a situation where she encountered the South African military. After reading it several times she responded, "as it is written… I would not want to be included in your book." She went on to express herself more fully and logically but the words *I would not want to be included in your book* kept playing in my head. I felt a warm ball of defensiveness in my gut. I sent an email back conveying my feelings of offense at her response and that I thought "I might not fall into your grouping of those 'white people on writing projects' given the depth and longevity of our relationship. I was mistaken. Thank you for making yourself clear." There, I felt duly justified in my feelings. Not so.

When I took a step back a couple of days later, I realized I responded as a typical white person. In my writing I had inadvertently interpreted Althea's experience of rage as a Black woman, something I knew nothing about on an experiential level. I had assumed the narrative from a position of power and then got offended when I was challenged.

Althea and I had a series of follow-up conversations, some emotionally charged, with me at one point wondering if our relationship could sustain the strain. I felt defensive about my manuscript and all the time and energy I had put into it. But ultimately, I knew that any credibility my memoir had depended on the honesty of those who I wrote about and who had so patiently educated this white woman. Even more importantly, my relationship with Althea is integral to my life and the integrity of it depends on my ability to hear her heart, even the hard stuff… especially the hard stuff. We were able to hear each other and commit to ongoing work in our relationship.

This experience is so relevant to where America is today. Althea and I represent on a microcosmic level the struggle on a global level of the desire of some to rewrite history. "A history about the 'other' without a fuller understanding, appreciation, or awareness of or describing their lived and felt reality within -- this can be enraging for those, like myself, perceiving or experiencing being done to -- in a long history of being done to," as Althea so truthfully puts it. A history that obliterates the hurt, pain, and oppression of the powerless at the hands of the powerful allows the dominate culture to avoid feeling discomfort. One example of this is the evil theory propagated by some that slavery really was a good thing and that it benefitted Black people.

White anger, on the other hand, is seldom talked about although equally present. It manifests itself at its worst when it is dressed up and controlled and emerges from positions of power. Cold and seething rage motivated a white minority government in South Africa to maintain the oppressive and brutal regime of Apartheid for almost fifty years, empowered a white policeman in America to keep a knee on a Black man's neck for seven minutes while he was handcuffed on the ground, slowly dying, or fueled an insurrection to overthrow a democratically elected government.

This white domination of the narrative cannot be sustained. Equity means recognizing and promoting stories from those who have for too long have been silent or unheard. We need their voices. Marginalized groups that have experienced oppression are uniquely qualified to lead the way to a just society as they carry the scars and learned painful lessons about injustice. The thirst for justice for all burns strong in their breast.

As I write this memoir and relive my experiences with marginalized people, it reinforces the fact that those who have the most to say have the least opportunity to say it. Many are taken up with the task of day-to-day survival with few skills or time to put pen to paper and share their invaluable wisdom. But as things are changing and courage has inspired new and inclusive literature, we must not ban it, but instead embrace and incorporate a new message and work for a more just society that leaves no one behind.

When we left South Africa almost three decades ago, I carried the hope that life would get better for the vast numbers of people who suffered under the yoke of Apartheid. I hoped that the revolution we worked for would be an economic revolution as well as a political one. While I am reminded by my husband that South Africa is a new democracy and things take time, I am saddened by how little has changed for so many. Economic prosperity has come to many who previously were excluded by laws based on race, however there is a persistent battle by political and corporate greed to maintain power that excludes over eighteen million individuals living in grinding poverty. But this is not just a South African phenomenon: it is a growing global war, waged by the haves on the have nots.

Meanwhile, I have witnessed over the years since my return to the States a frantic race to maintain power and control of a country that is changing. While this race has long affected many marginalized communities, largely communities of color, a new brazenness has evolved. Never has our country been more divided. "Christian moral values" are being politically manipulated to support bigotry and hate for those who are different on one side, and those who believe that all humans deserve justice and human rights on the other side. This fracture has divided families and communities. People who fear the growing diversity in our population have fanned the flames that the "other" is the enemy. White supremacy advocates exist in every echelon of our society, manipulating the fear, and emboldening the "foot soldiers" to act. Anxiety and fear seem to be driving the narrative, and I question whether love and justice can overcome these driving forces.

There is a Buddhist teaching that love and fear form the basis of everything. There is a biblical verse that states, "perfect or mature love casts out all fear." In other words, every act we as humans do is either an act of love or an act seeking love often out of fear of what we are missing. Fear of the "other" is a perception that they are taking something that belongs to us. Those who fear change and progress use the phrase, "We need to take our country back." This mentality distorts the reality. It is counterintuitive to the concepts of *ubuntu* and community. The priority of love is genuine love for myself as a person, "warts and all" as my husband says. I believe we came from love, distorted by life and all the things that happen to us, and this self-love restoration is our life's work. For me it is God, for others whatever their Higher Power, through the Spirit (Sophia, the female Wisdom) within us we can grow this love to maturity. It is a constant process. History is replete with examples of prophets and prophetesses who exemplified this:

Mahatma Gandhi, Harriet Tubman, Mother Theresa, Martin Luther King, Steve Biko, the list goes on.

My life continues to lead me to various places where I have the choice to cross the line into unfamiliar and uncomfortable territory. Even after leaving the formal work force, I have been asked to support persons of color as they encounter workplace racism and trauma. I now live in a very conservative, white, right-wing area of Lancaster County. I travel through corn fields and pass Amish horse and buggies, and homes with plain Mennonite folks and black cars to get to my lovely, wooded enclave where Graham and I share a home with independent living space with my daughter, son-in-law, and granddaughter.

At first, I struggled with finding peace amid all that I thought I left far behind me. But now I see I am just where I need to be. Because of my childhood, I understand the mentality of the plain Mennonite folks: I have been where the conservative white folks are. And so, I chat with the young Amish woman at the farm stall, while inside my heart breaks as I wonder what she will become. Will she ever realize the desires she may have, and does she know how beautiful she is and all that she is capable of? I call out a hello and wave to the lady who lives beside me with the "God, Guns, and Trump" flag flying high in her front yard. She waves back, and we discuss the beautiful evening, and she shares regret at having to go to work. I plan to make cookies at Christmas and share them with all my neighbors: I haven't done this in years but feel it is time.

And before you think I have gone all quiet and passionless… I woman the voting polls as a poll greeter for the Democratic Party. For the first time in years in my small town, those who come to vote will see two tables at their polling place: not just one to encourage the registered Republicans but also those courageous enough to vote Democrat. The first time I went to vote, the poll worker lowered her voice and said, "you know they have you down as Democrat." I assured her this was correct and went to vote.

I attend pro-democracy rallies and carry signs advocating for better health care and other justice issues. I plant my progressive yard sign firmly, front and center, informing all who pass that Black Lives Matter, Love is Love, Science is Real, etc.... I wear my progressive T-shirts when I go to pick up my granddaughter at kindergarten, amid the cornfields and back country roads. And I smile.

I made sure I showed up at the school board meeting where my granddaughter is starting school. The public school that she attends has a group of moms that represented Moms for Liberty, an ultra-conservative group that has been identified by The Southern Poverty Law Center as one of the largest hate groups, with Pennsylvania reportedly having the largest membership. They planned to attend the meeting to advocate for book banning and sanctioning the librarian. Together with my son-in-law, I attended and monitored the situation. Turns out the right-wing group seemed surprised by the opposition to their agenda and were pretty quiet. I have no idea how fierce the conflict could get, but I stand ready to cross over into uncharted waters in the pursuit of justice.

In a recent conversation with a dear friend, I was explaining what I was doing since I retired. I said how I wanted to stay involved in social issues and I ended by saying, "I don't feel I need to save the world, but I want to stay engaged." She responded, "Dorcas, you have already saved the world, you just need to take it easy now and enjoy life." I know she said this with all the best intentions, and I love her for it.

However, as long as I have breath, I will advocate for truth and justice. Even as the years take my physical strength and my voice grows weak, life to me always means there is an opportunity to grow. Growth means renewing the light and pushing back the darkness. It forces me to look deep into my soul and find those places where love is absent. It shines the light where pride and arrogance remain. Individuals patiently, or not so patiently, continue to help me strip those masks away. I believe that love and kindness are organic to our souls. It is up to us to do whatever is necessary to roll back the cover of our fear and cross the line into the redemptive process of love. I do not say this lightly, but I say it with the reality that it is our only hope.

Althea and Jurgen Banda-Hansmann in Cape Town

The Cyster family on a return visit to Cape Town in 2003

White Coats for Black Lives demonstration in 2020 during the Covid pandemic after the George Floyd murder. With hospital co-workers left to right: Dorcas, Maria, Beth, Dina, and Zipporah.

Acknowledgements

The ink was not dry on the last page of this memoir before I thought of all the others who have taught me so many more of life's invaluable lessons and whose stories need to be told somewhere. Maybe in my next book.

My mother whose life was changed so radically when she married my dad. I know you had a whole other life in you, somewhere. I have inherited your love for people and interest in their lives. You remain a memory to many women who remember your loving encouragement.

My siblings each have their own story. They have encouraged and supported me in various ways to continue this project that has taken almost a decade to finally complete. We are different in many ways and my journey has finally taken me to a place of peace and acceptance for each one of you. I love you all.

To my South African family who accepted me into the Cyster clan. I know you did not always understand this white American woman, but you shared your love freely. You continue to be part of the tapestry of our family life here in America.

My heart is full of appreciation for all those I have met along the way who represent the voiceless and often marginalized of our society. Those who are caught in generational poverty and oppression and yet warrant their story told as they work tirelessly to love and raise their children and serve others in their own communities. From the streets of Jackson, Mississippi to the back roads of Cape Town, South Africa, I have felt your fear, anger, and love and incredible wisdom and hope that has put me to shame and challenged me to be better.

Thank you to the editor of this manuscript for your work and believing in me. When I doubted if anyone would read my book or if my writing was important, she would encourage me with her words of encouragement. "You have a powerful memoir," she wrote. You have no idea, Margaret High how you kept me going.

My two beautiful, intelligent, and strong daughters who have taught me so much about life. They are as different as the parents whose genetics fused to create them. You are my legacy and all the good that has come from my journey is my wish for you. I love you both.

And finally, my soulmate, my impetuous and always loving husband who would tell me to keep going. You are a "word smith" he would say. Thanks for putting up with my moods when the reminiscing of memories exhausted and aroused strong emotions within me. I am indebted to the challenges we faced together and turned to gold.

About the Author

Dorcas Horst Cyster is a passionate advocate for physical wellness with a career spanning over 40 years in healthcare, serving as a Nursing Assistant, Licensed Practical Nurse, and Registered Nurse. She completed her bachelor's degree in Nursing at 60, reinforcing her belief in the intersection of emotional-spiritual health and physical wellbeing, further nurtured through her training as a Spiritual Mentor. She has been recognized with Nurse Excellence Awards and as a Woman of Achievement by the YWCA Lancaster PA. Now retired, Dorcas remains a social activist and mentor, while enjoying reading, yoga, and outdoor activities. She is a proud mother and grandmother.

(She can be contacted at deecyster@yahoo.com)

Milton Keynes UK
Ingram Content Group UK Ltd.
UKHW030755121124
451094UK00014B/1172